SECRETS OF SOBRIETY
©2021 Robert Edwards

Photography: Elaine Burrell

ISBN: 978-1-09837-877-6

SECRETS OF SOBRIETY

from

THE ROAD LESS TRAVELED

ROBERT EDWARDS

I would like to dedicate the book to my wife Ginny. It was through her effort I became involved in recovery. We share the same date of sobriety and a wonderful love.

FOREWORD

When Bob Edwards asked me to write the forward for this book I was honored. What an opportunity to give back, however small, to a man who so influenced my life. I first met Bob 22 years ago when I stumbled into the rooms of A.A. doing a ninety and ninety, ninety meetings in ninety days, desperate to stop my drinking. I could not believe that my life of accomplishments had led me to seeking help from A.A.

I was a career Navy Pilot with over 5,000 hours of flight time and 156 combat missions. With my engineering background the Navy provided for my postgraduate education as well as Senior Executive Training at Harvard. I enjoyed the responsibility of multiple commands as well a Service reputation that fed my ego. After retiring from the Naval Service, I progressed quickly in a Managed Healthcare Company to become its Chief Operating Officer. Yet there I was drinking a liter of Vodka a day and becoming morally bankrupt. I was a man who had lost the capacity to feel gratitude and was spiritually empty.

One of the meetings that was close to home was an all-men's Step Study meeting started by Bob Edwards. In there I found men of all backgrounds and many with long term sobriety. But more importantly I found men in fellowship dedicated to not just their sobriety but traveling a path to become better men and in service to others. Bob Edwards was our unofficial leader then and today and remains as the mainstay of that wonderful fellowship.

In that meeting I saw men who had not only abstained from alcohol but had something I never experienced in my life. They demonstrated at each meeting a calmness, acceptance and peace that had eluded me for 52 years. Bob was ten years ahead of me in his sobriety, but he was decades ahead of me learning to live a more spiritual life and grow to become a better man. Through the years together we have totally changed our live.

Many may question, do we need another book on A.A.'s success? On merit alone Bob E's three and a half decades of sobriety, commitment and service is a story worth sharing to others. However, this book is so much more. Few men I have met have demonstrated more courage overcoming adversity and tragedy, few have endured such good and bad cycles of fortune and few have so unselfishly give of themselves to help other alcoholics. Bob's story is not unique to us alcoholics. We have heard so many, but this book, "Secrets of Sobriety" is a wonderful addition to A.A.'s continuing story.

I most strongly recommend reading "Secrets of Sobriety" as it is an authentic depiction of A.A.'s power to improve the quality of our and our families lives and of those who have shared the "road less traveled" called recovery from the disease of alcoholism.

Ken Curtis

Captain, USN [Ret]

ACKNOWLEDGMENTS

I acknowledge the contributing authors as their quotes appear. Any original thoughts I might believe I had, without doubt, were influenced by those I have encountered in the thousands of meetings I have attended, in the enumerable materials I have read, and on the Internet, and by those who have come before me.

INTRODUCTION

I am Bob, an eighty-five-year-old alcoholic. This is my story, but in this story is much of the story of every alcoholic—their obstacles, their answers, their failures. Herein lies many of the secrets of a road less traveled, a narrow road toward freedom from alcoholism.

The word *alcoholic* defines me well, yet I am thirty-five years without any alcohol in my system. This condition, as you may be aware, is known as *sobriety*. Alcoholism, as you may not be aware, is a disease and, surprisingly, it may be the deadliest disease of all! Certainly, it is among the most challenging.

Unfortunately, there is today no known medical "cure."

Most diseases are well known, some serious, some minor, and many in between. Some are physical such as coronary artery disease, stroke, COPD, cancers, diabetes, and others. Some are mental such as anxiety disorders, depression, PTSD, and more. Medical doctors handle the physical ailments; psychiatrists treat the mental disorders. Neither handle alcoholism. Alcoholism was not successfully treated until eighty-five years ago, and it was not diagnosed as a disease until 1956.

Until then, the alcoholic was basically ignored. Then, in 1935, the Alcoholics Anonymous program was formed.

This is that story.

Through this writing, I attempt to explain alcoholism, my alcoholism, recovery, my recovery, sobriety, my sobriety, and the Alcoholics Anonymous program.

Why?

Although alcoholism is mostly hidden due to the shame of the disease, one of eight Americans is alcoholic by definition. *That is 12.7 percent of the population in the United States.* This is according to the *Diagnostic Manual of Mental*

Disorders, Fifth Edition [DSM-5]. The American Psychiatric Association declared alcoholism a disease in 1956.

Twelve point seven percent of the US population—that is more than 40,000,000 people!

Additionally, each abuser of alcohol affects many others.

In my view, alcoholism is therefore a worthy subject. I trust I am worthy of it.

ALCOHOL USE AND ABUSE

Normal alcohol consumption in the United States is one drink a day for women, two for men.

Abusive drinking begins at four drinks per day for women, five for men.

Binge drinking begins when the above occurs five times per month.

Alcoholism is defined here as impaired control over alcohol, preoccupation with its use, and continued use despite adverse consequences.

The effects?

Damage to the vital organs. Mood and behavior disorders.

Devastating effects on the brain and central nervous system.

Memory is affected. Alzheimer's disease is common, especially among women.

Liver damage is normal, as are dependency, depression, and anxiety

As important, family and friend relationships are seriously damaged, and professional consequences are common.

What can happen?

Disease, hospitalization, incarceration, loss of family and home, and death.

As you shall see, I was given a year to live at one time and a 1 to 3 percent chance of death at another. I was jailed twice and imprisoned once for a white-collar crime. I hurt my family and was bankrupt twice. I lost millions of dollars for myself and caused severe financial loss for others.

I developed companies worth many millions.

I am a member of Mensa.

Abnormal?

Alcoholism is no respecter of rank or privilege.

Feeling qualified, I shall continue.

For fifty years, I traveled the broad road of life. I have experienced the pleasure and the pain of those periods. During those years, I exchanged humility of birth for pride and arrogance—normal behavior, I believed, for who I was to become. This also is the story of my next journey, my thirty-five years of traveling down the *road less traveled.*

This road was my recovery from the disease of alcoholism. During these travels, we shall encounter the story of early Alcoholics Anonymous as it has revealed itself to me in thirty-five years of sobriety, and as it has influenced me.

I tell my story in the hope it might benefit those to whom my experience, my strength, and my hope might be useful, especially those who have had a need to use alcohol or drugs as an answer to life's complexities.

I direct this especially to those who have a rising desire to learn the history of the principles of Alcoholics Anonymous (AA) and those responsible for them, not to the historians by whom I have been influenced, or to those writing an academic paper.

Instead, I direct this book to those who may have a desire to stop drinking, to the average alcoholic and addict, and to whoever may have a desire to know more about AA, recovery, and alcoholism. To them I hope the reading may be of benefit—additionally, may it benefit whoever might have an honest curiosity about how recovery and the AA program work. To them I offer those "secrets of sobriety" I have learned.

It is important that you realize as you read that recovery from the disease of alcoholism was the most important event of my life: more important at that time than my marriage, my children, my spirituality, my health—even my life—as I would have none of these without my recovery. Now my marriage is the most meaningful thing in my life.

Read slowly! *Speed is no asset if you are going in the wrong direction.*

CHAPTER 1

HOW IT STARTED

I began this book, which I named *Secrets of Sobriety*, when I had about twenty years of recovery, more or less fifteen years ago. I became interested in what had occurred in my recovery and why. I believed I needed to learn what was responsible for the miracle of my recovery. I found I needed to understand the disease of alcoholism, and therefore I decided to learn about the programs responsible for my recovery.

The AA program, the subject of recovery, those responsible, and the details of those events and those involved are the basis of much of *Secrets of Sobriety*.

Alcoholics Anonymous may not be the only route to sobriety, but I think of an admonition of Will Rogers: "If you pick up a cat by the tail, you learn a lesson that can be learned in no other way."

Perhaps my recovery without the AA program would have been the same. The AA program was my introduction to recovery, and after many years, I determined to find more details of that program, although after twenty years in AA, I felt I knew the program well. I was wrong. My research showed my ignorance, and I began to use new resources to learn more. It was years again after that time that I felt I was competent to share my knowledge. The writing began, although I was not thinking of it as a book to share.

I let a few trusted AA members read my "work" to this point, originally concerning the beginning of AA, and they complimented me on the content. I then shared the work with a doctor friend, perhaps the most intelligent person I know. I had helped his brother to recover from alcoholism. He said it was interesting to him but boring to someone not involved with the program. He suggested I add personal details.

This, my story of recovery, is what I have chosen to add. Also, I recall, early in recovery, an old friend in the program telling me I should write a book, as my life, in his view, was extremely interesting. I have considered these suggestions and have added a simple biography. More on this story later as he, Alfred Heck, authored three excellent books.

This, my story, was not happening in a vacuum, but years passed before a book became a possibility. I was learning about the characters in the history of recovery. I was growing interested in the sequence and the details of the AA program.

I was committing all my writing to drafts as journaling, and only later to a combined form. A real problem was becoming apparent. Over time, I had four areas of thought, all quite interesting, but with no sequence for readability as my interests changed over the years. I realized each part of the writing might have been useful, but the writing lacked enough continuity to be compelling to a person who needed recovery or who might have a strong interest in alcoholism.

I needed a magnet to pull it all together. What did I have? What had I learned? In retrospect, I realized I had concentrated on different areas of recovery as my program progressed. How to integrate them? They represented different areas of progress without regard to when they became part of who I had become and who I was to become. My program at thirty-five years of sobriety was different than my early program. I believe my growth should be demonstrated only as I grew. Still later growth may show up in my writing about my early recovery before it was learned. The story of my early program might demonstrate the effect of later learning as I write.

Please also be aware this book was written in four major parts, with no thought of it becoming a book. Nevertheless, occasionally each part may contain information from another part. Kindly be patient with my duplicity.

In the AA program, when describing our recovery, we are to tell what it was like, what happened, and how it is now.

With this as a loose format, I shall begin. First again, an introduction.

CHAPTER 2

INTRODUCTION

I am eighty-five years old as pen touches paper. Thirty-six years ago, at age forty-nine, I was given a year to live, likely due to my abuse of alcohol and cigarette smoking. Nevertheless, I changed no habits. I continued drinking, as the disease of alcoholism, as you shall discover, is so strong.

I did quit smoking—my wife and I quit together. It was more difficult for her than for me. A year later, at age fifty, for reasons to be discussed, we both entered recovery from the disease of alcoholism. I credit the AA program for my recovery, as you shall see. Alcoholics Anonymous keeps no membership roll, and for reasons of anonymity, I am requested not to identify as a member.

Thirty-five years later, I am alive and doing well. Doing well, however, includes several consequences from smoking for twenty-five years and from excessive consumption of alcohol: chronic obstructive pulmonary disorder (COPD), ventricular tachycardia, atrial fibrillation, sleep apnea, and high blood pressure, not to mention what I call old guy stuff (OGS).

I am bionic—surgeons have implanted an automatic installed cardiac device (AICD), commonly known as a defibrillator-pacemaker, which electronically transmits my heart condition 24/7 to Johns Hopkins Hospital on the East Coast. The installation was complex, during which I was given a 1 to 3 percent chance of survival (there is a story here). Interestingly, it was more than a year after surgery before anyone shared that information with me. I credit the disease of alcoholism, with no thanks, for these disorders.

SOME BACKGROUND

I now have a marriage of more than half a century. I have a relationship with a son who begged his mother to divorce me. Although I am not wealthy, money is no longer a problem. The promises of the program (more later) have materialized to an almost embarrassing extent.

I walk by San Diego Bay every day. I work out at a marvelous spa three times a week. First, I walk and do warm-ups, then I lift weights in the gym. I do many repetitions with substantial weights. Five years ago, the weight was double, and I was training for the Senior Olympics in the sprint. My COPD put closure on that goal.

My life has been rich with experiences for which I, my family, and others have paid a high price. For reasons to be discussed, I became an alcoholic. I cannot say when I graduated from heavy drinking to alcoholism—nevertheless, I have earned the label *alcoholic*, and by it I am accurately defined, although I am thirty-five years today without alcohol in my system. *Alcoholism has no cure, only remission.*

My first journal, of which there are now four, was the beginning of this book. This was circa 2005, about sixteen years ago as I write. These "secrets," as I term them, slowly evolved as my life progressed, and I believe they must appear to you as they appeared to me: slowly, or as I recalled them.

Secrets are not at first apparent. Be patient.

Each journal was inspired by the subject I was then most interested in, first the AA program, then its effect on my life, and thereafter its synthesis. The chronology is imprecise. The biography of my life, much of what I have learned, and many of my life experiences are included in this book.

Be prepared for content rather than style.

At the time of writing, as noted earlier, I had about twenty years of sobriety, I had absolutely no alcohol or drugs in my body, and I was beginning to believe I may have something to contribute to those interested in alcoholism or addiction. Since that time, through many efforts, I have increased my knowledge of the disease of alcoholism, which is of addiction, and of recovery. Every day brings a more complete understanding of the disease, but I am faced with the fact I shall not have an infinite future toward better understanding. I must, for that reason, contribute that which I now can, or it may be all forever lost.

I shall present these secrets as they occurred in my life. This is not an indication that I became aware of the depth of these new understandings as they occurred.

I did not stop drinking and become immediately wonderful.

I became, as new information came available, aware of a new understanding that required new behavior. Therefore, each new awareness required deeper understanding and rethinking old behaviors. This required time.

CHAPTER 3

SOBRIETY AND ITS ELEMENTS

Secrets of sobriety, our subject, require an understanding of sobriety and therefore of alcoholism and recovery. These secrets of sobriety cannot simply be listed. These secrets, when first encountered, as noted, merely open the door to a requirement for new behaviors while rethinking old beliefs.

All this will, therefore, be encountered in a simple biography of my life, during which time these "secrets" will appear at the speed with which I realized them. As you become aware of my life and recovery, you may also become aware of these secrets.

You may not, of course, be fully aware of the consequences of alcoholism, codependency, and addiction—this I shall attempt to correct as we progress.

Alcoholism will be properly covered as we go forward, as will codependency and addiction. These are large subjects that require much information to be digested and then properly understood.

These secrets of sobriety are primarily directed toward recovery from the disease of alcoholism. I shall attempt to organize these "secrets" by sequence of occurrence, although this may be difficult and may not have practical importance.

NOTICE.

Needing personal recovery is quite different from having curiosity about recovery. Needing recovery and being willing to do that which is required calls for a different attitude toward learning.

Recovery is honestly responding to those biases encountered in life, which we have absorbed in the experiences of our life,

My solution was to become a student of AA and later Al-Anon. I hope this reading may also benefit you—additionally, may it benefit whoever might have honest curiosity about how the AA program works. I offer those "secrets" I have learned along the journey of my recovery, or, as Scott Peck would say, the road less traveled.

CHAPTER 4

Sobriety, and as I choose to term it, the *secrets of sobriety*, are not defined in current medical or psychiatric literature. These disciplines favor the term *abstinence*. The term *abstinence* is found in medical and psychiatric literature and is generally agreed upon as the treatment for alcoholism and especially severe alcoholism. *Abstinence* is defined as the nonuse of the substance to which a person is addicted.

The difficulty in selecting the nonuse of alcohol or drugs as a solution to life's complexities is that alcohol and drugs are cunning, baffling, powerful, and also patient. On my own, the attainment of "sobriety" has proven nearly impossible for reasons I shall attempt to explain. First, alcohol or drug use in excess changes the body's chemistry and creates a need for alcohol to keep the body's chemistry in balance. Additionally, it causes a mental dependence.

CHAPTER 5

I shall introduce you to AA's *Big Book*. In the *Big Book* is an important chapter outlining the importance of how it works, which is the chapter's title. This is a portion of chapter five of the *Big Book*:

Rarely have we seen a person fail who has thoroughly followed our path. Those who do not recover are people who cannot or will not give themselves to this simple program, usually men and women who are constitutionally incapable of being honest with themselves. There are such unfortunates. They are not at fault; they seem to have been born that way. They are naturally incapable of grasping and developing a manner of living which demands rigorous honesty. Their chances are less than average. There are those too who suffer from grave emotional and mental disorders, but many of them do recover if they have the capacity to be honest.

Our stories disclose in a general way what we used to be like, what happened, and what we are like now. If you have decided you want what we have and are willing to go to any length to get it, then you are ready to take certain steps.

At some of these we balked. We thought we could find an easier, softer way. But we could not. With all the earnestness at our command, we beg of you to be fearless and thorough from the very start. Some of us tried to hold on to our old ideas and the result was nil until we let go absolutely.

Remember that we deal with alcohol—cunning, baffling, powerful! Without help it is too much for us. But there is one who has all power— that one is God. May you find Him now. Half measures availed us nothing. We stood at the turning point. We asked His protection and care with complete abandon. Here are the steps we took, which are suggested as a program of recovery:

1. We admitted we were powerless over alcohol—that our lives had become unmanageable.

2. Came to believe that a power greater than ourselves could restore us to sanity.

3. Made a decision to turn our will and our life over to the care of God *as we understood Him.*

4. Made a searching and fearless moral inventory of ourselves.

5. Admitted to God, to ourselves, and to another human being the exact nature of our wrongs.

6. Were entirely ready to have God remove all these defects of character.

7. Humbly asked Him to remove our shortcomings.

8. Made a list of the persons we had harmed and became willing to make amends to them all.

9. Made direct amends to such people whenever possible, except when to do so would injure them or others.

10. Continued to take personal inventory and when we were wrong promptly admitted it.

11. Sought through prayer and meditation to improve our conscious contact with God *as we understood Him,* praying only for His will for us and the power to carry that out.

12. Having had a spiritual awakening as a result of these steps, we tried to carry this message to alcoholics, and to practice these principles in all our affairs.

Many of us exclaimed, "What an order! I can't go through with it." Do not be discouraged. No one among us has been able to maintain anything like perfect adherence to these principles. We are not saints. The point is, we are willing to grow along spiritual lines. The principles we have set down are guides to progress. We claim spiritual progress rather than spiritual perfection.

Our description of the alcoholic, the chapter to the agnostic, and our personal adventures before and after making clear three pertinent ideas:

a. That we were alcoholic and could not manage our own lives.

b. That probably no human power could have relieved our alcoholism.

c. That God could and would if He were sought.

You must have noted the need to understand who and where you are, the need for honesty, and the willingness to change.

"How It Works" is read at the beginning of each meeting.

As you may now have some insight into the AA program, I shall continue.

As I determined to write this story, I went back to old sources and read and reread them all. I secured and read new sources on the subjects pertaining to the history of AA and the men and women and organizations important to AA as we know it today. The Internet has been invaluable. Through this process I have been introduced to the depth of my ignorance about alcoholism, of which I had thought myself knowledgeable.

The story of AA and obtaining sobriety is detailed and includes many important people and events, and the order of events as I present them may be imprecise. I shall attempt a balance for ease of comprehension and for the broader readership with the understanding that addiction and alcohol are no respecters of position, intelligence, age, or length of sobriety.

It is important to understand these secrets and this information will not reveal themselves or be of importance to a mind presently influenced by alcohol or mind-altering drugs. For these writings to be somehow useful to an alcoholic attempting sobriety, a point must be reached where alcohol or mind-altering drugs no longer influence your reasoning.

Taking all of this into consideration, I will introduce to you the author by telling my own story in order to give you an understanding of my physiology, my intellect, my genetics, and the environment in which I was raised, by whom I was raised, and that by which I was influenced.

You need to be able to compare who I was and who I am now in order to evaluate the information I present. Although I am not an Einstein, I am not at the lower end of the bell curve of intelligence; this needs to be considered as age, experience, interests, and intellectual capacity all have a strong influence on perception.

A secret of sobriety

I have no real desire to tell my personal story. I do so as I have come to understand that some who might benefit from the story of AA and its secrets would lose interest without a personal element included. I hope my story fills this need.

To discover these secrets of sobriety, you must follow my experience in recovery. Let us begin by traveling the entire length of the road less traveled. As we travel, mindful that we are attempting to understand alcoholism, we shall follow AA's method of sharing—that is, how it was, what happened, and how it is now. Additionally, I will explain what I have learned and perhaps also why it works.

CHAPTER 6

HOW IT WAS

My early years were rather normal for an alcoholic. My father was college educated, had a master's degree in math and education, was a coach of all sports, and had been a star in almost every sport while in college. After college, he became a coach, was a par golfer, bowled 300 numerous times, and was on a state championship baseball team. He actually boxed professionally and successfully for a time.

My father was an amazing athlete. He was thirty-five before he met an athlete who could outrun him. I have seen him make one hundred straight free throws on the basketball court. (During those years, free throws were mostly thrown underhanded, and although not illegal, this is seldom seen today.) *I was, on the other hand, moderate in these abilities.*

My father returned an alcoholic after serving in World War II, although he may have been drinking on an alcoholic basis earlier. I was, of course, not aware of this at my early age. My father was a bar drinker and was seldom at home after work until late in the evening.

My siblings and I therefore may have avoided some of the problems of growing up in an alcoholic home. I did not have as much stress at home as did some children of alcoholics. Again, I was to become aware of this only much later in life.

Instead, my brothers, my sister, my mother, and I experienced a lack of overt love and caring from my father. We lacked money in the home, but our mother experienced that lack more than did we. I compensated by beginning to work by age eight. Again, we children were not aware of our father's lifestyle being different from that of other fathers until later in life.

My own son, having been in the AA program for ten years, has done the same. He is an expert at getting jobs and earning his own money. *His goal as a young man was to be as unlike me as possible; he encouraged my wife to divorce me. It was years after my recovery before we repaired the relationship.*

My mother seemed to be the backbone of our existence. She displayed to us children no hint there was a problem in our home. Later, when we began to see for ourselves that our life was not normal, we believed the problem lay with our father.

He was the alcoholic!

Only when we were fighting the disease ourselves (my youngest brother was in AA with thirty years of sobriety before his death) did we find there was in our father's family almost no alcoholism; however, in my mother's family alcoholism was rampant. The subtleties of this distinction are not easily apparent, although when the families of both parents have histories of alcoholism, the statistical probability of alcoholism in the children increases.

A secret of sobriety

During the writing of this book, the admission of my activities during the years of my disease has been unexpectedly difficult. This comes as a surprise as I have shared all of my history, my defects of character, and my past misdeeds in thousands of meetings; nevertheless, it is proving very painful to once again relive the events and to put on paper the person I had become. Perhaps this is because I am so content in my new life.

The transition from who I was to who I am now was enormous. Within that transition is this story. My personal interest, after many years in the program, had become the history and dynamics of AA. This interest, I have come to understand, is not shared by all, and many probably have little interest in AA to the extent of my own fascination with the subject. Perhaps my life may hold your attention. I have been urged to tell my story for years with no connection to my alcoholism. I shall say more on this later in the book.

As I attempt this personal history, I am finding it exceedingly difficult to recall all the details of my past and affect a precise chronology; an understanding of denial might help you understand this issue. As I have already acknowledged, much of my history is painful to share and memorialize. Additionally, I had accepted a version of incidents in my life that was "gentle" toward my behavior. I am sure "huffing" has been present. Be aware. Alcoholism, though, touches the lives of an enormous sector of our US population and of the population of the world, and therefore I choose to put aside my own feelings.

First, I include a brief biography of my own life until the time of my becoming sober, and later of my life after initial sobriety.

CHAPTER 7

IN THE BEGINNING

I was born on a farm in Central Texas in a tiny town called Rochelle on August 23, 1935, in the same country farmhouse my mother had been born in twenty-one years earlier. Actually, I was born in the very same bed.

My parents were both new teachers, together earning about $100 a month. In the summer, they went to college at Howard Payne College in Brownwood, Texas, almost the geographical center of Texas. My mother's father's name was William Wilson; my mother's maiden name was Lois Wilson. At the time I was not aware of the coincidence—these were the names of the cofounder of the AA and his wife. I was named after my father's father, Robert Edwards, Bob, the county judge. Much of my childhood was spent on my mother's parents' farm in the country near Rochelle.

The house was not painted and a porch spanned its entire front. The exterior boards around the house were also the interior boards. The large front room was lightly furnished with a hodgepodge of items. Next came the combined kitchen and dining room, although we did not think of it as a dining room but as part of the kitchen. The kitchen was the best part of the house in my memory. The house had only two bedrooms as I recall, and a covered back porch that acted as a bedroom also. The house had no running water, electricity, or outhouse. Certain necessities were performed behind the chicken house, where corn cobs had other uses. Light in the evening came from kerosene lamps. My father's family was upscale in comparison, with an outhouse and last year's Sears Roebuck catalogue rather than corn cobs.

I did not think of the front room as a living room. We had a battery-operated radio to which we listened only on Saturday nights. I recall Franklin Roosevelt's fireside chats, and have memories of Amos and Andy, Fibber McGee and Molly, and Orson Wells's famous broadcasts.

I loved the farm. I had uncles, aunts, and cousins to play with. The extended family was so large the ages of grandchildren and children overlapped—I had cousins nearly as old as aunts and uncles. I had a cousin the same age as one uncle.

My grandmother and my older aunts cooked breakfast each morning: biscuits and gravy with bacon or sausage. Those breakfasts and Sunday dinner were my favorite meals. We called the noon meal dinner. We had plenty of eggs from our chickens. There was no refrigerator or even an ice-box, just a box in the window draped with a wet feed sack around it to keep food cool. Peanut butter was a special treat, and it lasted without refrigeration. I called it "pea buddy," according to my Uncle Tom. Flour came in fifty-pound sacks—the sacks were made of good cotton cloth with different designs on each bag; these became our shirts, and the ladies sewed the remnants into quilts.

My grandfather let me ride with him on the farm equipment, behind a mule and a horse. The barn had a haystack next to it. I would climb onto the top of the barn and jump into the haystack. My grandmother caught me, my brother, and my cousin doing this, and she came and gave us a good whipping. She said it ruined the haystack; nevertheless, it had been great fun. Whippings were administered with a slender, limber branch from a young tree or bush, and "spankings" were not infrequent.

In the evening, the grown-ups would sit on the front porch as we children chased fireflies and put them in mason jars. We played games and had a great time. Sometimes the younger uncles and the older cousins would pull our pants down to the great amusement of the grown-ups on the front porch and to our shame.

A creek satisfied our water needs. We carried the water from the creek in buckets to the kitchen. It provided a great swimming hole below where we got water. Before I learned to swim, my grandmother gave me a one-gallon syrup bucket inside a feed sack to paddle with. I remember the creek flooding all the way up to the house. We found it exciting.

It never occurred to me we might be "poor"; I did not understand nor had I ever heard the term *poor*. We lived just like everyone we knew except the townspeople, who were somehow mysterious. We had hot biscuits each morning and sausage or bacon from our own hogs and eggs from our own chickens and milk from our own cows. We had fried chicken on Sundays. The town kids had "light" bread for their sandwiches (packaged loafs). This made them "rich" in our eyes.

For Sunday dinner, my grandmother would choose several chickens and (skip this if you are queasy) wring their necks and leave them running around with no heads and flopping on the ground. She or my aunts would then put them in boiling water to make it possible to take the feathers off. Then the chickens would be cut into pieces and deep fried in lard. The lard came from slaughtered hogs. The youngest kids got wings and legs. Thighs went to the next oldest, and breasts went to the adults only. Kidneys and livers went to the weird ones.

I watched, fascinated, as my grandmother milked the cows and squirted milk to the cats. She could aim. Farm animals such as dogs and cats had their own responsibilities, and we were not as attached to them as many are to their pets today, although I recall the farm dog was a cocker spaniel named Sadie. The cats lived in the barn and fed themselves. I do not recall any of them with personalities. We did not play with them.

Our beds were shared, boys with boys, girls with girls. As I had twelve aunts and uncles, I do not recall where everybody slept; of course, as there was such an age difference, all were not there at one time. The quilts were handmade. Homemade, we called it. I do not recall anything about sheets. My grandparents' bed had a quilt-sized frame over it, hanging from the ceiling. The neighboring ladies would come over and lower the frame to their level, sit around it, and sew scrap material into quilts, and they gossiped, I suppose, about the things women talked about in those times. Each bed had a chamber pot under it for nighttime purposes. When it was cold in the winter, we had cloth-covered bricks to keep us warm. It was about 1938; I was three.

CHAPTER 8

My father's parents lived in West Texas on a farm near Rule and were by some standards well off. They had a John Deere tractor rather than horses and mules. We called the tractor "Popping Johnnie." It was so named as it had only one large cylinder with the resulting pop, pop, pop noise from firing on only one cylinder. To keep the engine's momentum, there was a large, heavy external flywheel. The flywheel also served as a power transfer by applying a belt to it and onto another piece of farm equipment such as a buzz saw.

There was a windmill for water. We had cows and hogs and chickens. There was a little building called the smokehouse. Its purpose was curing meat by smoking it. Whole hogs hung upside down in the smokehouse. We milked the cows for our milk and cream. A machine called a separator brought the cream to the top with the richer milk. We churned butter from the cream. A churn was a three-foot-tall, heavy, glass-like cone with a smaller hole in the top where a pole with a plunger at the end was pushed up and down to agitate the cream and make butter. After the cream and whole milk came to the top, the milk remaining, today's nonfat milk, was fed to the hogs with the leftovers from our meals. We called it slopping the hogs.

Later, a milkman delivered our milk in glass bottles; the top several inches would be cream, and sometimes in the winter the milk would freeze before we got it inside, and the paper cap would pop up and the cream would rise an inch or so.

Cotton was the primary money crop on both farms, although maize and corn were also grown, and probably other things I do not recall. Maize and corn were fed to the cows, horses, and mules, and maize to the chickens; we also had vegetable gardens. My grandfather Robert Edwards, known as Bob, was also the county judge, as mentioned earlier.

When I was in first grade, I rode to school in a horse-drawn wagon and carried a bag of eggs that I traded for my lunch. The farm was several miles outside of Rochelle, which was small with a population of about two hundred. The population density was and is about two people per square mile. The county seat was Brady, miles farther, where the population was perhaps five thousand.

The population in Rule, Texas, is today 636. The population of Rochelle, Texas, is today about 163. I now live in the city of San Diego, California, with a population of more than a million, and as I look out my window at the time of writing this, I can see the aircraft carriers *Ronald Reagan* and *Carl Vinson*, both with crews of more than five thousand.

My grandparents on both sides had large families, twelve children on each side. Large families were the rule as they then had to hire no help and sometimes could hire the children out to those families needing help. Help was called "hired hands."

I had an uncle, Bailey Edwards, who could pull a bale of cotton a day, about five hundred pounds. There is a big difference between picking cotton and pulling it. To pick clean cotton, you have to pull the cotton out from the boll, whether by hand or by machine. Cotton gins were more primitive at that time and could not separate the bolls from the cotton. Gins are much more sophisticated today, and machines now pull much of the plant and clean the cotton from the plant. Picking cotton involves pulling the whole boll as more modern gins can accomplish the separation and much more. Therefore, you can pick much less cotton than you can pull. Uncle Bailey would straddle a row and "pull" the middle row and those on both sides. Modern cotton-picking machines "pull" perhaps ten rows at a time.

My father was young enough then not to be necessary around the farm as a field hand. He was a very gifted athlete and earned a full athletic scholarship to Howard Payne College. While a student he excelled in football, basketball, and track, as previously mentioned. We lived later with my father's family until my father got a position as the principal of a three-teacher school in West Texas equidistant from Rule, Haskell, and Stamford, my father's family home area. It was named Center Point. We lived there three years. The school employed a male and a female teacher as well as my father; my mother was not yet accredited. All three families lived in a four-room "teacherage" on the school grounds. There were four rooms and a "path." The path led to the outhouse. There was a well for water, which was drawn up by buckets as there was no water system. They had to carry water from the well to the house. The school was also our church with student pastors from Hardin Simmons University in Abilene, the nearest large city.

School was in session except when it was necessary to chop or pick cotton. Chopping cotton involved thinning the cotton plants until they were about a foot apart. When the plants matured and the cotton was ready to pick, school would let out and all the students old enough to do so would pick cotton. I had my own small "cotton sack" at age six. During the summer break, my father worked as an undertaker's assistant and my mother went back to college.

The teacherage stove used kerosene, and as this was the Depression, our neighbors, who were poorer than us, would often steal it. They would also siphon the gas from our car and, as there were no gas gauges in cars at that time, it was easy to run out of gas. Housekeeping was difficult, a washeteria was miles away, disposable diapers were a thing of the future. The washing machines were the wringer type and laundry was rinsed in a tub. There were no dryers, just clotheslines. My mother's family's farm had no facilities at all—all clothes were washed at home. Few clothes were ironed, but when there were clothes to iron, ironing was done with an iron heated on a stove.

Dad was very sports minded, so we went to many ball games. I attended my first college football game at age six weeks. This was in Brownwood, where my parents got their undergraduate degrees. My brother Jim was born there in 1937. Jim died in 2021 during the COVID-19 pandemic. He would have been eighty-four in twelve days.

My mother went to school that summer, and my father worked in San Angelo and played baseball for two teams, one of which won the state championship. Dad pitched and caught; he was particularly good, a very gifted athlete.

At the end of the summer, my mom had enough credits to earn her teaching certificate, and she began teaching the primary grades. The next fall, Dad went back to school and got his degree at midsemester; teachers did not have to have a degree to teach, but they did need to be accredited according to the standards of that time.

The last part of the year, Dad taught at a little school named Indian Gap. We lived in a little rock house on a hill. His oldest brother, Robert, an accountant, was killed. He was returning from playing golf with friends. They were riding in a dump truck and wearing golf shoes with steel cleats, and he slipped in the steel bed and fell. My grandfather went into a long depression.

The next school term was my dad's first year as a coach; the school was in Rochester, Texas.

Our next school was in Rotan, Texas. That school had a particularly good football team, and my dad's coaching career was improving each year. He was ambitious and wanted larger and better schools. My brother Mack was born there in 1940. I was five years old. Mack died of cancer in 2018, after he had achieved thirty years of sobriety.

The entire football team was the right age for the draft when World War II broke out. One member of the team became a fighter pilot and was killed over Germany. Another was killed in Britain; another was a casualty when his carrier was sunk. Casualties were often in the thousands at each battle. The newspaper often had entire pages full of the names and hometowns of the casualties.

My mother's brother Fred was in the army. He went missing in action and was not heard from for months until a mailbag was found floating in the ocean. He was on the Bataan Death March and was a prisoner of war for three and a half years. Her younger brother Richard had been a gunner on a ship until a shell hit the gun turret and he was killed. Another brother survived the war, but suffered severely from what we know today to be post-traumatic stress disorder (PTSD). He later wandered away from home and family and died alone.

My father had not been drafted as he was married with three children. However, as the war progressed, it became apparent he would be drafted. He chose instead to enlist and joined the Marine Corps. This was 1942. I was seven.

While my father was in the Marines, we moved to army base housing. The base was named Camp Swift and was between the Texas towns of Elgin and Bastrop. In the Marines, my father became a rifle instructor and was sent to the South Pacific. I do not know what his duty there was, probably in reserve for being sent to the front. The end of the war prevented that. Importantly, the Marine Corps taught him to drink, or at least was instrumental in the progress of his drinking. Prior to this time, alcohol was not a problem in our family to my knowledge, although I am certain alcoholism was in its early stages at least.

During the war, my mother got a job at Camp Swift at the base post office. Camp Swift, as mentioned, was between Elgin, population today of eighty-five hundred, and Bastrop, Texas, population seventy-five hundred today. Austin, the state capital, is about twenty-five miles from both towns with a population approaching nine hundred thousand. This is in Central Texas.

We boys of school age were bused to school in Bastrop and had no real supervision as our mother was at work in the post office on the base and my father was overseas in the South Pacific. I recall slipping with my pals onto the Camp Swift base rifle range and climbing through a concrete-lined "ammo" dump, where unexploded ammunition and grenades were thrown. I suppose we were lucky to have survived rather than becoming some of the youngest casualties of World War II.

We loved this time of our life; we were surrounded by kids our age from all over the United States. The base housing area was rural and we dug caves, made rubber guns, and generally had a great time. Even with no supervision we were good kids. I developed an aversion to school and was not a good student, but I was already entrepreneurial. Fleer Double Bubble gum cost a penny and was extremely popular and not very available; I would buy an entire box and would sell the pieces of gum one by one for a little profit. I also was approached by a local dry cleaner. I picked up clothes from around military housing and delivered them to the truck, which came every several days. I was paid a small percentage.

I was about ten when the Japanese surrendered in 1945. I clearly remember the celebration at base housing. I beat on a pan with a big metal spoon. There was a big party around the central office area. My father had been in the South Pacific for the balance of the war. When he came home, it was midsemester, and to get work, he took a job as a tutor for two children on a huge South Texas ranch. The ranch had a four-story house that to me was enormous, and barns and many other buildings and sheds. The owner was an exceptionally large and wealthy woman; however, she did not look or act rich to my eyes. The fourth floor of the house was empty except for racks of new dresses that were large and plain.

The property was so huge the railroad had to go through it. The property owner gave the railroad right of way with the provision that it had to throw her a newspaper each day, and she could stop the train if she chose to go to town.

She had a boy and a girl our age, so we had good guides to the property; they loved having us there. I think they were lonely. She owned a Palomino horse worth $25,000 and a bull that won first prize at the Houston Livestock Show and that may have been as valuable or more. I have no idea why I remember the values of the animals (or if these values were correct). We had horses to ride, and it was an exciting time. It was 1946. I was eleven.

In the fall, my father went back to coaching with some success, but a new element had entered our lives; although as youngsters we were not aware of what it was or its cause. The drinking habit he had learned in the Marines was now an everyday part of our life. Although we were a bit too young to understand, I am sure it influenced us.

In 1946, we moved to a new school in East Texas. The town was Arp. Arp is near Tyler, a city of ninety-six thousand in northeast Texas, and is known as the rose capitol of the United States. Arp was an oil town. My father had his first major success as a coach in Arp; he had the highest-scoring basketball player in the nation, Bunky Bradford. His assistant coach went on to coach the Houston Rockets.

By age twelve, I was driving, and I would drive the maid home in our 1946 Oldsmobile. No new car models had been introduced since 1941 due to the government taking all the cars for the war effort.

Next, we moved to a little farm town in East Texas named Purdon. Purdon was a big downgrade in schools for my father as they had no sports except basketball. My father's drinking was beginning to affect his ability to get hired by better schools

My sister, Jan, was born in Corsicana, the largest city near Purdon, in 1950. She is fifteen years younger than me. She only weighed four pounds and ten ounces; I weighed nearly thirteen pounds when I was born. Of course I was weighed on a cotton scale and the weight may not have been precise. The high school in Purdon had only four seniors and offered general math only every other year. It was so small that as a freshman I was named the "Best All-Around" boy with a half-page picture with Genetha Grinstead, the "Best All-Around" girl in the school yearbook, *The Dragon*, which was a full forty pages long and nearly a quarter inch thick. Although the only sport was basketball, we did have a gymnasium.

My father's first basketball team did not have a gymnasium but an outdoor basketball court. My father's team won the district title game, which was played in an indoor gymnasium. One of his players was interviewed about playing indoors. He said it is easier playing indoors as you do not have to allow for the wind.

As in the other farm towns, school was interrupted in the spring as all the kids had to chop cotton. Chopping cotton, as previously noted, was done to allow a space of about a foot between cotton plants. I chopped cotton with all my friends—it was extremely hard work. School started late in the fall as we had to then pick cotton. I picked cotton, also hard work. The farmer was at the trailer when we brought our full sacks to be weighed and emptied. He inspected our cotton to make sure it was clean. We added a rock to our sacks for more weight as we were paid by the weight we picked. The cotton was later taken to the gin. I recall with embarrassment that a girl, Daffin Putman, a junior, could pick more cotton than me. She could pick two hundred pounds a day.

My parents bought a 1949 Chevrolet, the first new model introduced since 1941 and the first new car we ever had. We had a nice house with a separate garage. There was an indoor bathroom, although there was no bathtub or shower. Water came from our own cistern, which is a round water reservoir made of galvanized metal designed to catch rainwater. It was raised to produce a gravity force for running water. We bathed once a week in a double-sized tin tub in the kitchen; mother got the first bath as the water was the hottest and cleanest, then my father, then my brothers and me. The water was never changed and looked gray by the time our turn came to bathe. Jan was tiny and did not need a big bathtub. I could put her head in my hand and her feet only reached my elbow.

The one-car garage was of simple construction with a dirt floor. The outer walls were also the inner walls and were of 1 x 8 x 8 planks and attached at the top nailed to a wooden 2 x 4 frame with a simple roof. The bottom was also a frame of wooden 2 x 4s, which also went across the opening at the bottom front. The floor was dirt.

Purdon was often wet. The soil had clay in it and was slick. One rainy night, I was given permission to park the car in the garage. I was still an inexperienced driver and was anxious to prove I was careful. I approached the garage slowly and then the rear wheels came to the wooden 2 x 4 plank going across the front, where the rain had created a puddle.

When the tires came to the puddle and the 2 x 4, the car lost traction in the mud and the tires started spinning. As a new driver, I was confused: why wasn't the car moving? I checked that the engine was running; it was. Next, I checked that the car was in gear—a manual three speed, of course it was in gear. That exhausted my theories as to why the car was not moving. I got out to see if the problem was outside. At that time, the car gained traction and jumped into the garage, then through the back of the garage. As the bumper hit the wall low, it popped the nails at the bottom and the top nails held. Thus, the car went through the garage and outside and the boards fell back into place.

The garage looked entirely as a normal empty garage should look. But I had to chase the car as it chugged down into the field below. My father heard the noise and looked out the window to see the car disappearing into the field. The rear of the garage boards was back into place and the garage looked totally normal. Normal. The same was not true of my reception inside the house. I never told my parents how it happened.

In Purdon I began building model airplanes with gas engines and learned to fly them. It was the beginning of a lifelong love affair with airplanes.

The Purdon school system contributed to my lack of proper schooling. There were only four seniors. General math, as I said, was offered every other year. No algebra or geometry or science.

Our next school, as Dad's drinking was becoming even more of an issue in getting work, had no sports and offered only grade school. This was in Manchaca, just outside of Austin. My brothers and I were bused to Austin to school. Jan attended grade school in Manchaca. The schools in Austin were particularly good; the high school was a 4-A school, the largest category in Texas. I was far behind all other students my age. I had been able, to this point, to do the schoolwork with my natural intellectual gifts; this was no longer the case.

My father now had a famous bar as his home away from home, The Tavern in Austin. There he drank every day with many well-known Austinites, including sportswriters, President Lyndon Johnson's brother, Sam, and others. Here began a serious gambling habit, or here I became aware of it. During this time, with his sports knowledge, my dad did so well gambling he caught the attention of whoever operated gambling in Austin: the Mafia, we thought. Whoever it was, they sent out some very tough guys to discourage my father's winning gambling. He took me with him, and we met them in a bar near the University of Texas. They scared him. They scared me too.

Sam Johnson lived in a downtown hotel. He was a drinker, not unlike my father. My father, although his drinking influenced his work and his home life, was highly regarded among his friends such as Sam Johnson, many rich friends, professional athletes, sportswriters, and other newspapermen.

Sam Johnson had wonderful clothes, some of which he gave me. The heavy cotton shirts had removable collars and cuffs that were attached with little wooden dowels. This allowed different colors on the collars and cuffs. I cut the sleeves off to better show my "muscles." It was 1951. I was soon to be sixteen.

My father's drinking and womanizing had earned him such a poor reputation it was difficult for him to secure a position in a good school. Nevertheless, he got a good job in far West Texas, a little town near El Paso, Fabens, where his reputation apparently had not reached. He spent two successful years coaching there, but his drinking and carousing again cost him his job.

While in Fabens, I became a well-known sprinter and was not beaten until I reached the regional relays in Odessa, nearly four hundred miles from Fabens. West Texas is not very dense. I ran the 100-yard dash and the 220-yard dash, and I anchored the 440-yard relay. The two teams in the relay that beat us in regionals came in one and two at the state meet; nevertheless, I had to stay home as only the first two team winners went to state. One of those teams became the state champion. My brother Jim, now deceased, was to later to become an accomplished half-miler. We were only somewhat good, not great. My father, when he was a college athlete, won the college division in the 100-yard dash and the mile run at the Texas Relays, a major national event. This was an exceedingly rare feat. This is my recollection. Later, as earlier noted, he would bowl 300 many times and become a par golfer. He was an exceptional athlete. He was thirty-five before he met a student athlete who could outrun him, as previously mentioned. Later he coached the top hurdler in the nation, Don Beard.

While in Fabens, I began to develop a reputation as a fast and reckless driver. After football practice, I drove some of the Mexican players home. I drove so recklessly they told my father they could not play football if they had to ride with me. This was a difficult situation for me as my father was the coach.

I was on the football team but not first string; I had to develop a name another way. My reputation was "bold." After a football game we won, I drove to the other town, climbed the water tower, stood on the rail above the walkway, and painted the score on the tower. This was Clint, Texas.

As a junior I began to drink, but I was not aware of the damage drinking can do and had already done to our family. Drinking was easy for a teenager, as no age limit was enforced in Mexico. Juarez, Mexico, was just over the border from El Paso, just twenty miles away, and the border and a smaller town were less than three miles from Fabens. Whisky was fifteen cents a shot and prostitutes were $3. What a perfect environment for a potential alcoholic to be in! I did not think of myself as different from my friends as we did the same things. I was to learn my dedication to these new habits was stronger than that of most of my friends. I graduated from high school at age seventeen. In August, I would be eighteen. It was 1953.

CHAPTER 9

The summer between my junior and senior years I was hired by a contractor that paved highways. The first job was about one hundred miles from El Paso in a town named Dell City; we had to drive the equipment there. My vehicle was a pneumatic roller, a heavy roller filled with concrete blocks and dirt for added weight; it had twelve tires designed to compact the gravel and dirt before the asphalt was applied. The "roller" was pulled by an Allis Chalmers tractor. The next machine to compact the surface was a very heavy machine with two huge steel drum rollers filled with water. This machine did the final smoothing job on the asphalt. We called it a steamroller.

The Allis Chalmers tractor reached a top speed of about eight miles per hour. Nevertheless, I had to drive it one hundred miles to the construction site near Dell City. On the way to Dell City was a mountain road called 40 Mile Hill. I got bored after a while driving eight miles an hour. The tractor had a hand clutch, and I would disengage it and let the pneumatic roller go a little faster downhill. Unfortunately, I let it get too fast and the clutch would not hold the machine back. The brakes had no effect, and faster and faster I went. The vehicle that was balanced at eight miles per hour became very unbalanced at the speed I had attained, and I thought it was going to shake to pieces. Finally, I exceeded thirty miles an hour and passed my boss in his pickup. My only option was to drive it to the bottom of the hill. My reputation was made.

My pneumatic roller was filled with dirt to add weight, as just mentioned, and I added a small rattlesnake I had found. We lived in tents on site during the week. We had a cook for our meals who served giant flapjacks for breakfast. I loved it. We drove back home after work on Saturday. I hit overtime on Thursday. My salary was $1.35 per hour; I thought the salary was enormous as I got more than $2 an hour on overtime, which usually occurred on Thursday morning. The boss thought we were a wonderful crew.

When the Dell City job was completed, I was transferred to the plant back in El Paso, where a rock crusher crushed rock into gravel, which was mixed with asphalt as a base for the product we called "hot mix." The crushed stone was loaded onto a dump truck that then dumped it onto a central pile, which finally got to seventy-five or eighty feet tall. A dump truck would have to back up the hill of gravel and dump its load of gravel at the top so the "clam shell" on the crane could pick up the gravel to load the trucks. When the pile got too high, I was called on to back the dump trucks to the top. I was chosen for this job, as to get to the top you had to back up as fast as the truck would go, and most of the drivers could not or would not back up that fast. One day, on the way to the top, the crane operator swung a load into my truck and wrecked the truck.

Back at school in Fabens, I managed to graduate with decent grades and chose to go to college in El Paso at Texas Western College, now the University of Texas at El Paso. My father had a new job in Central Texas, but I was able to live with my maternal grandparents, who had moved off the farm in Rochelle to El Paso years earlier.

Their son, my uncle Tom Wilson, was an employee of the Mountain Bell telephone company in El Paso, and with his help I secured a night job in the garage, servicing trucks at the end of the workday. A friend from high school worked for Southwest Air Rangers in El Paso on the weekends. He got me a job there, and I worked twelve-hour days Saturday and Sunday as well as a forty-hour week for the telephone company. This was in addition to college. I began flying then, and spent the whole paycheck from my weekend job on flying.

I was not a careful pilot, but very bold. I remember looking at a giant, white, puffy cumulus cloud. It must have reached more than thirty thousand feet into the air. I decided to fly into it to see what it was like. In the cloud, I decided to level out. I had no reference. Every position seemed the same, as it was all white up, down, and sideways. I was not trained in instruments yet and could not read the instruments to achieve level flight.

I did understand the airspeed indicator, and as I looked at it, I saw I was going over 165 miles per hour, a dangerous speed for that airplane, a Piper Tri-Pacer, which was cloth covered. I came out of the cloud upside down, pointing straight toward the ground. I did know what to do then and all became well.

I remember on a cross-country flight I was leaving the mountain area where the mountains were about four thousand feet high. Just over the edge was a drop of several thousand feet. On the mesa at the top was what appeared to be a dry lake, which looked like it would be safe to land on. I had seen some caves as I went over the top edge, and I thought I would land and explore them. I lined up on the dry lake to land, and as I leveled out to touch down, I could see the airplane was not responding in the manner I was used to. It was the thin air at the high altitude. I barely made it over the edge and was again back in control. I had just learned an important lesson in flight. Luckily, I survived.

CHAPTER 10

I failed to consider that college might also require time. As it happened, college was more than I was prepared for. I had studied no algebra, no geometry, and little science and was ill prepared for college. Nevertheless, I enrolled in the school of engineering as that seemed to be the masculine thing to do. I quickly learned my math and science background was woefully inadequate.

Although I was to learn I have a high IQ, I did not have the proper background for engineering, or for college at all, actually. I was ill equipped to do college work. Years later, I took the Mensa test, and scored a high enough IQ to join Mensa; nevertheless, natural intelligence, although enough for most of the schools I had attended, was not adequate for college-level engineering work without the necessary academic background.

I found not a few other students had as much natural intelligence as I did, and years of advanced math and science. My English skills were also well below average. I was required to attend adult school to take more algebra, geometry, and physics, as well as to study technical drawing to equip me to do the engineering work required.

I had an enormous schedule to which I added a social life that included Juarez, Mexico, just across the border. A full-time job, a twenty-four-hour-a-week part-time job, and a poor school record was more than a Mensa IQ could overcome.

CHAPTER 11

The Korean War caused a need for pilots, and the US Air Force changed its rule that had required a college degree to enter its flight program. It now required a test for which I was qualified, as it was concerned who I was—bold—rather than my poor academic background.

Aircraft at that time were simple with no radar, sonar, or global positioning equipment. Pilots therefore were not required to do much more than to learn to operate the airplane successfully. Their job as fighter pilots was to chase or avoid enemy aircraft and to shoot them down.

My daredevil lifestyle fit the test used in those years. I passed with a nearly perfect score, 96 out of 100, and enlisted in the US Air Force to await my class assignment. It was 1955. I was twenty. While awaiting my cadet class, in order to avoid being drafted, I was required to enlist in the regular air force and go through regular basic training. I became a squad leader, my first promotion. Rather than doing all my own work, making my bed, arranging my locker, etcetera, I found the best bed makers and had them make all the beds. All the other jobs were also done by those most skillful at those particular chores. As a result, my squad always finished first in basic training competitions, but my airmen also perhaps did not learn some necessary skills. It never occurred to me many of those men did not ever learn to make their own beds or arrange their uniforms or keep their area neat. This might be an insight into my persona.

My cadet class finally began. The first portion of cadet training was officer preparation and, upon graduation ninety days later, class officers were selected by a board consisting of instructors, officers, and peers. I was selected as Group T and O, a captain's rank, and was second in command. My air force career was off to a good start.

Primary flight training was in Kinston, North Carolina. Our class was to be the last to fly the Texan Junior, or T6 as it was best known. The T6 was already twenty-five years old when I trained in the old war bird. The navy called the T6 the SNJ, and one is on display on the *Midway*, carrier #41, based in San Diego, California. It was appropriate this was to be my aircraft as it was the last of the "low tech" trainers. We began training in a Piper Cub, the PA 118, which was a simple cloth-covered, two-seat, tandem, high-wing airplane. I had already had training in more advanced airplanes and was the first to solo.

I also had my first incident; I was caught doing a loop in the instrument area for which I received a reprimand, although it was secretly applauded as it demonstrated my "fighter" attitude in the view of my instructors. Looping in the PA 118 was considered dangerous because if you did not have the airspeed to complete the maneuver, the PA 118 could fall through on its empennage (the tail section). As the airplane was covered with cloth, this could tear the section off. My loop, however, went well.

My training went mostly very well, although I was only average in instrument flying. While I was in instrument training, my instructor threatened to "wash me out." He was a very salty old navy pilot who was extremely skillful. He would get angry at me and take the stick out of the rear cockpit and beat me over the head with it. Luckily we wore helmets. I did not respond well to his type of instruction. I would later learn I have attention deficit hyperactivity disorder (ADHD), making it difficult to concentrate and focus, especially under that type of pressure.

My instructor, Bear Edwards, gave me an ultimatum—change instructors or he would eliminate me from the program. Of course I opted for the change in instructor, and my new instructor was young and low key. The change was perfect for me, and I blossomed under his tutelage. The next phase of training was a series of landing stages with six landings in each stage. Three of the stages were normal landings, another stage was five thousand feet power off, another was night landing, and the final was power on.

The scoring was as follows: landing within fifty feet of a marker in a three-point position and maintaining the three-point position (no bouncing) achieved a score of 1 per landing. Missing the marker, landing too early or too late, and not maintaining a three-point position increased your score according to the magnitude of the errors. An excellent score was 12. Remarkably, I scored 6 on all the normal stages and night landings, 8 on the five-thousand-feet power-off stage, and 11 on the power-on stage. I was informed that was the best score ever attained over the many years of the program. I now had a reputation complete with attitude.

I discovered members of the air force band received an evening of liberty. I rushed down to try for cymbals, which I believed were simple enough to master. Unfortunately, someone beat me to them, so I tried for the drums, those with soft tips on the drumsticks, which I also thought perhaps I could master.

Alas, the drums were also already taken. Finally, my only option was snare drums, which I elected to try. As I was underclass, I was last chair, and I found I could blend in with no noticeable disruption. I even got good. I had to listen carefully as I did not have the advantage of being able to read music. I simply had to blend in, which I managed.

All went well for months. My first major problem occurred when a general arrived and we had a parade that involved marching while drumming across the tarmac. To my embarrassment, I dropped my drum and had to chase it across the runway. Also, unfortunately, when I turned upper class, I was in now first chair. During upper class graduation, the piece we were playing had a long pause during which I drummed away. My cover was blown. The band leader said, "Mr. Edwards, you are not able to read music, are you?" Found out.

I survived that incident, but I did not survive what came soon after. I owned a yellow 1951 Mercury convertible and enjoyed liberty and the attention from having beer at a local drive-in where I was well known and believed myself popular. On the fateful night of my demise, a Saturday evening, I was talking to girls at this hangout. I knew girls there well and was using language not unusual for the situation. Suddenly a stranger in mufti (civilian clothes) approached me and attempted to correct my language. I reacted, as was my habit, in such a way the stranger responded, "Do you know who I am?"

I, of course, responded, no doubt under the influence of alcohol, and protecting my position in the eyes of my peers, "Not only do I not know who you are, I don't give a damn" (Rhett Butler, of course).

The stranger was a brand-new graduate of West Point and entirely new to the base—it was his first day. He had no exposure to cadets, student officers, and officers sharing the same instructors, the same classrooms, and the same amount of respect, treating each other as equals. He turned me in the next day for insubordination. A condition existed at that time where some airmen had acted badly in town and the town was asking for "a head." It was to be me.

Additionally, there was a reduction in force (RIF) in the military due to the fact that the Korean War was winding down. The military took the easy way out, and because of a technicality where I had enlisted for two years to await my class assignment, I qualified under the RIF. The RIF stated that if there was less than two years left on your enlistment and you had not progressed beyond your permanent grade of Airman 3rd, you became part of the RIF. It was 1956. I was twenty-one.

CHAPTER 12

THE UNIVERSITY OF TEXAS

All my dreams were down the toilet. I was devastated. I went back to Austin and enrolled in the University of Texas. My other option was to fly for American Airlines for under $500 per month, and my GI Bill payments compensated for much of that. Another factor in my decision was that I was thoroughly brainwashed against multi-engine aircraft. I was not enthused about "driving a bus," which I considered multi-engine aircraft to be.

My years at the University of Texas (UT) were satisfactory. I enrolled in the school of education, where I was better suited by training and aptitude. I was not an excellent student, but my grades were entirely satisfactory, even good, a B average. I did well in the biological sciences, English—especially writing where I equaled the highest score ever awarded—and, oddly, in drama. I studied water safety at UT and became qualified to train lifeguards. The first summer, I took a job as a lifeguard at Barton Springs, a world-famous natural swimming pool in Austin.

CHAPTER 13

As the summer ended, a UT professor, who swam there most evenings and who oversaw the Defense Research Laboratory at the University of Texas, approached me with a job offer. He and several professors had started a company named TRACOR, which was to become a huge national company. I accepted. My early job with TRACOR was preparing a super clean room, essentially painting every surface, in order to produce intergraded circuits, microchips (chips).

I held a very low-tech position in that company, but I also worked as a guard at the Defense Research Lab. One of its facilities was a floating platform on Lake Travis near Austin. One evening, I dropped the time clock in deep water and had to retrieve it. I had to learn to dive with SCUBA equipment, especially at that depth. On the bottom, I located the time clock right next to a huge catfish, probably well over fifty pounds. I gave it the respect it deserved.

TRACOR in its early days had little money, and the president, who had hired me, offered me twenty-six hundred shares of stock in lieu of my unpaid salary. His name was Frank McBee. I asked him instead to pay me when he could, which he did. Those twenty-six hundred shares later came to be worth $3.7 million. He teased me about it years later. I told him I would have sold when the shares were $5—even then I always needed money with no thought of the future. That was my first "million dollars." It was now 1958. I was twenty-three.

CHAPTER 14

MY NEW CAREER

My GI Bill benefits were about to expire, and I became aware that the starting salary for a teacher was $5,000 a year. I had a year left to graduate, and I elected to enter the workforce rather than continuing university. (I finally graduated at age sixty-two.)

In May 1958, I went to work for a major insurance company, where my talents served me well. I passed everyone in my division, which included the whole state of Texas, in production in only eight months. I was also in the top ten in the entire company. I was immediately promoted to manager and did well as a manager. It was 1959. I qualified for the company convention in Miami. I was twenty-four.

CHAPTER 15

MARRIAGE AND BOSTON

During the company convention in Miami, I met my wife to be, Kathleen Marie Lopez. Kathy's family is Italian, but when the first member of the Lopes family came to Ellis Island from Sicily, the immigration official assumed the name was Lopez rather than the Italian Lopes. The family retained the spelling and became local meat merchants.

I had been told promotions were easier to obtain for married employees. I therefore married; again, that was who I was. My promotion took me to Houston, where I again qualified as a manager for the next convention, which was held in Washington, DC.

My first child, Robert Russell Edwards, was born in Houston during the infamous Hurricane Carla. Dan Rather was the local TV announcer, and due to the week of national coverage of the hurricane, he had his start to a distinguished career in television. It was 1961. I was twenty-six.

My wife was from Boston and wanted to return there in order to be near her family. It was beginning to be noticed that I was poor at handling money. I took the opportunity for a change, and we moved to Boston, where I elected to go to a much bigger and higher-quality company, Massachusetts Mutual. My sales and management skills provided a job as a sales agent.

My drinking was becoming an issue, although I still did not realize it to be a problem. I was drinking every day and had begun gambling. I was beginning to emulate my father. It was 1962.

I had a wonderful situation in Boston. I had purchased a beautiful condominium. One of my fellow agents later became president of Mass Mutual, and I was in a good position to advance. His record was little better than mine. He had an advantage, however; he was married to the daughter of the general agent of the largest agency in the company. He had been furnished the doctors' market, the most lucrative market at that time. I felt respected in the company, by my general agent, and by my peers.

My lifestyle meant making money was beginning to be a problem, however. I was living over my head, influenced by my belief that tomorrow my income would soar. I would hit a home run. It was not to be. My energy had switched from work to my drinking habit. I did not understand the disease of alcoholism. I was beginning to choose friends who drank like me. It is a common behavior to choose alcoholic friends. Your self-esteem is comfortable with friends similar to you.

A secret of sobriety

I became a fan of the Boston Patriots, now the New England Patriots, and saw the first game famous quarterback Joe Namath played in. I also enjoyed the Red Sox baseball team.

At one particular Red Sox game, I sat in row two between home and third and had a hot dog ready to take the first bite when Mickey Mantle hit a foul ball directly at me. I put up my hands to catch it and my hot dog exploded over my face and the faces of my neighbors—mustard, bread, and meat were everywhere. I pretended it was not me.

A tragedy occurred that had nothing to do with my drinking: my condominium blew up. The cause was a natural gas leak. Everything we owned was destroyed except that which was on our back or in our car, a Mercury Turnpike Cruiser convertible—again, a car chosen to enhance my ego and self-image. An interesting story emerged from the explosion. A little friend of my son Rusty wanted to come and see him just before the explosion. His mother, for reasons unknown, refused his request, but he slipped away anyway and was just across the street when the house exploded. He believed it to be his fault and was terrified. I understand he required a bit of psychological help.

We received almost no financial help from our insurance or the gas company's insurance, and in order to compensate for my need for money, I forged the signature of a policy owner for a temporary source of money. I was not able to repay it on schedule and was found out. This was another example of needing money and acquiring it however I could, with every intention to repay it. I was fired. My wife divorced me. The divorce was caused more by my drinking than by the event; nevertheless, I blamed others for my misfortune.

A friend I had met through the Kiwanis Club gave me a job. He owned a rental equipment company and he befriended me. He paid for my evenings out with the club and for my golf. To repay him I took money, perhaps $10 or $20, from the company till. I financed a gambling habit I had acquired, going to the dog track. Finally, I chose to return to Texas. I owe my friend Bob Cameron, owner of North Shore Rentals, an amends. I have not been able to locate him. This was 1966. I was thirty-one.

CHAPTER 16

BACK TO TEXAS AND MARRIAGE TO GINNY

I returned to Austin. A wonderful event began to unfold; I met my wife to be, Ginny. From the moment we met, we were inseparable. She and I were both rebounding from a failed marriage, and each filled a need in the other. I taught her to drink with me and we did so every night.

I returned to work at my old company. I started back as an agent and again set production records, once selling 218 single policies in one week. I was quickly promoted and was in the process of another successful year when I again used company money and was audited and again terminated. I believed it was bad luck because of course I meant to repay it from my next check. I had not yet accepted the fact that my actions were not acceptable in the world of business, and in fact I was acting illegally and could be jailed. Out of work again, I was able to get a job as the manager of a prominent boating company, the Longhorn Boating Club on Lake Travis.

By now Ginny and I had decided to marry. We impulsively decided to elope as our plans for a traditional wedding ceremony grew complex, and we drove to Laredo, Texas; Nuevo Laredo, Mexico, was just over the border. We arrived on Saturday evening, March 24, 1968. We sought someone to marry us, which we believed would be simple. It was not to be so. In Mexico, weddings were usually performed in the church, mostly during the day on Saturday.   Conventional ceremonies in Texas are performed by a justice of the peace, but in Mexico, marriages are simply registered by a *juzgado civil*, the title of the local Mexican judge.

No *juzgado civil* was available on a Saturday night in Nuevo Laredo, and Sunday we began driving south into the Mexican state of Nuevo Leon. In city after city we tried to find a judge until we reached Monterrey, a major Mexican city hundreds of kilometers from the border. With no luck at all we started back north toward Texas.

We soon stopped at a police station in a little town where we met a young man who decided to help us. He told us there was a nearby *rancho* so large it had its own *juzgado civil* and he drove with us there. The hangout on that *rancho* on a Sunday morning was a small *cantina* on the property. It was perhaps twenty feet by twenty feet with a dirt floor and pigs and chickens wandering through. The judge was not present, but the entire bar was full of men who thought it an adventure and left to find him. Several hours passed, and we used the time drinking Carta Blanca, a Mexican *cerveza* (beer). As the men started returning unable to find the *juzgado*, we began to lose hope.

Finally, up drove a black 1946 or 1947 De Soto sedan with suicide doors, the rear doors opening front to back. Out of the back seat came a tiny man in a dark blue double-breasted suit. We saw he was *mucho borracho* (inebriated). He came into the *cantina* and asked for a sheet of paper, which he folded in two and tore in half. He then began asking questions, first of Ginny: where we were born, our parents' names, where we resided, etc. Then he asked the same questions of me.

He soon finished and asked for $25, probably more than $200 today, a large fee, we thought. We later learned it was due to Mexico raising money to pay for the 1968 Olympics to be held in Mexico City that year. The fee was so large Mexicans were coming to Texas to marry. Registration by the state is the legal definition of marriage in Mexico. Church weddings include this registration. We had only enough money to get home, so we had to send the money back to the judge when we returned to Texas. We did so and included $10 for the young man who assisted us. He said it was put into his daughter's confirmation fund. The registration ceremony was on March 24, 1968, and our certificate of marriage arrived several weeks later, dated April 5, 1968. The time between these dates we celebrate as our own little Mardi Gras.

CHAPTER 17

MARRIED AND BACK TO WORK IN AUSTIN

Back in Austin, I returned to work at the Longhorn Boating Club. On the first day back, I needed to take a new trimaran on its maiden sail. John Elliot, a star New York Jet footballer, was working for me. I paid John, as I recall, $5 per hour. He had just earned $7,500 for his role in the Super Bowl; this job was his recreation.

John and I planned to sail across the lake to test the boat's systems. Unfortunately, I had not installed pintles into the gudgeon plate, which is to properly affix the rudder. This allowed the rudder to slip out of its correct position. Off we sailed and as we gained speed, the rudder came out of the water. We therefore had no control of the boat; it increased in speed and a sponson dug into a wave and we pitch poled into the lake. I was thrown halfway up the sail.

We slowly drifted upside over to the opposite shore, more than a mile from the clubhouse. We were short staffed, and the incident was not noticed from the club. We signaled to no avail from across the lake; finally evening came, and we started walking back through the woods to find a ride back to civilization. The opposite shore, where we were "shipwrecked," was heavily wooded and uninhabited, but finally we came to a farm where the farmer was feeding his animals. After we helped him feed his animals, he agreed to drive us to a telephone, which was located in a country bar. We looked so disreputable, wet, and dirty, the owner would not give us anything to eat or drink until John agreed to leave his Orange Bowl watch as collateral. We finally got back to Austin late that night. This was my second night as a married man, and we were featured on television as missing and feared drowned. My reception upon returning was mixed.

As my salary at the boating club was small, to earn extra money I took a job managing a restaurant that was only a few hundred feet from the boating club. As Lake Travis is not a constantly level lake all the docks and installations are floating and adjustable to compensate. This was also true of the restaurant. The restaurant had to open by 6:00 a.m. to accommodate fishermen for their breakfast and "supplies," mostly beer and sodas. The restaurant had a pool table and a lively business selling beer. At noon we served lunch, primarily hamburgers. The Lake Travis Lodge Restaurant was a favorite hangout for drinking beer and playing pool in the evening. I could not afford help and had to do all the work myself. This required me to get there at 5:30 a.m. to open, and closing time was 12:00 on weeknights and Sunday and 1:00 am on Friday and Saturday. Including work at the boating club, this required a twenty-hour day. I drank lots of coffee and a lot of beer and played a lot of pool with customers. I have never worked harder or for more hours. I was not paid hourly but received a percentage of the profits. I do not recall making a lot of money.

CHAPTER 18

A NEW DIMENSION IN LIFE

My three children from my first marriage could visit Ginny and me in Austin. They got along famously with Ginny, and we were having a great summer. The oldest was Robert Russell, my first son and a great little guy. We spent a lot of time on the water. We had a small boat before my employment at the Longhorn Boating Club, and I taught him to water-ski. Rusty, however, was to meet an untimely death. More on that later.

Cynthia Marie was my next child. She has had an interesting life—she married a senator, earned a master's degree in science that she used for a teaching career, and now is a grandmother, substitute teacher, and snow skiing and mountaineering instructor in Lake Tahoe on the California– Nevada border.

My youngest child was Allison Frances, the absolute apple of my father's eye. He could hardly look at the other children he was so taken with Allison. Regrettably, she was killed in a boating accident just as she was entering nursing training.

One of the activities Ginny and the children enjoyed was coming to the lake and going out on one of our speedboats. One fateful day, they came out for an adventure. Ginny, Rusty age six, Cindy age four, Allison age two or three, and our young Mexican maid, who was about sixteen years old, came out to take a boat ride. I gave them a nice safe little runabout for their adventure. Toward the end of my day they had not returned, so I got in another boat and went out after them. I saw them across the lake and raced toward them. In my "hot dog" manner, I made a turn that would have me cutting right behind them, a typical spectacular Bob maneuver.

Unknown to me, the children were misbehaving, and Ginny had told the young maid to take the wheel while she settled them down. To the young, inexperienced girl, it seemed I was coming right at them. She turned into me, both boats were totaled and sank, and everyone was in the water. I evaluated the situation. Everyone except Rusty was afloat in their life jacket with their heads out of the water, screaming. I went to Rusty. His face was under water and he was not conscious, but I could see no injuries.

Other boaters witnessed the accident and soon came to our rescue. Everyone else got on the first boat and I took Rusty to the second one. A police boat with medics met us and I handed Rusty over to them. As I did so, he stiffened. I was to learn it was the first sign of brain damage. Of course my ex-wife Kathy came to Texas, and the balance of the summer was spent in recovery of the minor injuries of all except Rusty, whose brain damage, we were to find, was permanent.

The only light spot was that Ginny's eyes were so black from the boat wreck that the children called her the black-eyed witch, which they enjoyed. It became apparent that Rusty's brain damage was severe and permanent, and at the end of the summer his mother took him back to Boston. The children visited us each summer.

When Rusty entered puberty, he began to be aggressive. He had been a wonderful boy until the boating accident. Afterward, the medicine necessary to control his behavior had the side effect of altering his looks, and he became difficult to handle. He injured his younger stepbrother, and their family social worker made a decision to put him into a facility for children with behavior disorders. Before the date of Rusty's transfer to the "home," Kathy decided to take a final holiday with him to Lake Winnipesaukee in New Hampshire. While swimming, Rusty got into deep water and needed help. My daughter was there and told me years later she believed her mother had planned his death rather than have him taken. Rusty drowned at twelve years old. He was the first of three of my children to die, two by accident.

In the years after, life became relatively normal. Ginny worked as the manager of a large apartment complex, and during this time she became pregnant with our son Rhett. Ginny was tiring of the heavy routine and wanted to go back home to San Diego. My lifestyle was causing Ginny serious doubts about our marriage and she longed for the security of her birth family. Rhett was born and soon after we moved to San Diego. It was 1969. I was thirty-four.

CHAPTER 19

SAN DIEGO AND MY NEW CAREERS

Ginny's parents were well-to-do, and we had a wonderful place to live: a two-story house with a glass front overlooking the city, San Diego Bay, the Pacific Ocean, and Mexico. They adored Rhett and we had a happy time until my alcoholic behavior became a problem.

San Diego's economy was largely based on the aerospace industry, which was experiencing a depression. It affected the entire San Diego economy, and I was having difficulty getting work and even more difficulty affording my alcohol habit. Somehow I managed.

I compensated by drinking more than normal. I came in drunk one night too many, and I heard Ginny's mother say, "Ginny, you have married a common drunk." For the first time in my life, I was forced to examine who I was becoming. I found reasons to deny the truth. It was to become a necessary talent.

Ginny's father, on the other hand, was the real deal. He had been a college professor in Idaho and was now an aerospace engineer for General Dynamics. His intelligence and job skills were such that he was given the project of designing the life support system for the moon shot. He did so and was given a converted Boeing 707 to test the device by "shooting" parabolas. Parabolas are accomplished by diving to get necessary speed, climbing, then diving; during the top of the arc, weightlessness occurs. They achieved seventeen and a half minutes of weightlessness while testing the machine. He became the last aerospace engineer in San Diego for General Dynamics.

In San Diego, as I have mentioned, 1969 was a difficult year to find work as the aerospace industry was in heavy decline. In the interim I sold Amway and worked at a job placement agency on straight commission. Reverting to my entrepreneurial instincts, I devised an auto auction where car owners could sell their own cars from a central location. I called this the California Auto Swap Meet and hired the huge Del Mar Fairgrounds parking lot for the event. We had the Department of Motor Vehicles and all other services there to aid in transfer of titles.

It seldom rains in San Diego (less than ten inches per year), but it poured that entire first weekend. Nevertheless, we had to pay for the fairgrounds, which took all our funds and folded the operation. Other well-financed operations adopted the idea, and it is now a staple event in San Diego. Luck also plays a role in life.

CHAPTER 20

MY CAREER IN THE YACHTING BUSINESS

Although I made little money in job placement, I had learned to advertise my clients and decided to use this skill on myself. I called every yacht broker in San Diego and presented myself. I soon found work as a yacht salesman at the most prestigious company in all of Southern California. It was 1970. I was thirty-five.

I excelled, was soon given a private office, and outperformed the other salesmen's combined efforts. The sales manager believed the results were due to my office location, previously a gate hut to the yard, and hired another salesman to share my office. He was only moderately successful. He was, however, a retired navy captain and I learned much from him about ships and the sea.

Kettenburg Marine was a famous California chandlery and boat-building company. The Kettenburg sailboat line had been famous for more than twenty years. I learned every facet of the yacht business. I observed yacht equipment being sold and learned its function. I watched yachts being designed, built, and tested. The company built a fishing boat for Bernie Meyer, the Meyer of Metro Golden Meyer. It cost over $250,000, at that time, a huge sum to me. I went to Los Angeles to pick up his previous yacht, a nearly new Bertram 38, and went into his condominium on the water at Marina Del Ray. The playroom was filled with cases of tuna he had caught. He seemed a very ordinary guy. I was beginning to believe wealthy and respected men were rather normal.

Kettenburg was much more famous for its line of sailboats. I was there during the transition from wood to fiberglass. My knowledge was becoming extensive. While I was a salesman, the Whittaker Corporation bought Kettenburg and started a new line of boats, the K32. Whittaker resold Kettenburg and the line was dropped. I later bought the unfinished yachts and completed their construction and sold them all.

While I was at Kettenburg, Richard Nixon was president (1969–1974) and gave Nikita Khrushchev a Cadillac. In return Khrushchev gave Nixon a hydrofoil boat, a somewhat normal boat with foils under the hull that brought the boat out of the water and allowed it to "ski" on top of the water. President Nixon, who lived nearby in San Clemente, gave the hydrofoil to my boss, the famous Paul Kettenburg, to test its performance. Paul chose me to trial the little boat. The construction of the hydrofoil was very rough and typical, as I came to understand, of Russian workmanship. Their MIG fighter planes were designed to be throwaways—that is, not to be repaired but replaced as they aged. The United States, in contrast, rebuilds aircraft, some as old as half a century, such as the B-52 bomber introduced in 1955 and still flying.

My coup de grace at Kettenburg was a five-boat deal in which I sold a fifty-foot yacht with the understanding I had to sell the owner's fort-two-foot boat. I arranged a buyer for the forty-two-foot boat with the same stipulation: sell his thirty-five-footer. I did so to a man who was able to buy if I sold his thirty-footer, which I did. I ended up with the last two boats as a part of my commission. Another broker, from a very snobbish Newport Beach company, complained I had taken his customer. A high-level inquiry determined I had acted properly (and skillfully).

My son Nathan was born at this time. It was 1974. I was thirty-nine.

CHAPTER 21

OPENING MY OWN COMPANIES

After Whittaker sold Kettenburg, the company went into decline. I left Kettenburg, got my own broker's license, and opened my own company, the Yacht Company Limited. I had during this time become very capable in handling yachts, large and small, and began owning a few. By the time I left the yacht business, I had owned fifty-eight yachts up to sixty-five feet—not because I had an interest in owning yachts, but as the result of buying and selling for profit. The prestige of yacht ownership, however, fit the personality I desired.

CHAPTER 22

INTERESTING CUSTOMERS AND EXPERIENCES

I had many interesting customers: Robert Goulet's first yacht, *Le Bateau*; Jim Croce's wife, Ingrid, who purchased a sixty-five-foot sailing yacht; John Wayne, whose yacht was a huge, converted minesweeper named *Wild Goose* docked at his home in Newport Beach. In John Wayne's driveway was his Pontiac Safari station wagon; the front of the roof was raised at least six inches with a little window to accommodate his hats. Fernando Marcus, ruler of the Philippines, and his wife, Imelda, were customers, although I had nothing in stock to satisfy her. Her shoes were nice.

The company was hired to furnish several yachts and drivers for the *Harry O* television series, which was filmed in San Diego. I was the primary yacht driver and the interface between the film studio and the yacht company. David Janssen was the star of the program. I was able to get to know him rather well. He was very personable, and we talked a lot about guy stuff: cars, girls, etc. He was afraid of boats, and I had to drive except for brief close-ups. We started early each day and shot each scene sometimes over and over. The excitement soon wore off and moviemaking became boring. We had to do all shooting before about 3:00 pm as David usually became inebriated by then.

One scene depicted the police chasing the yacht I was driving. The scene required David (with me driving of course) to drive the boat up onto the beach just below the bridge in Coronado. I hit the beach at about thirty miles per hour. That was exciting! (The studio paid for all damages.)

I was impressed with the director of the series, Jerry Thorpe. The studio would fill the boats with cameras and technicians. The forward hatch was removed and a camera was located there facing aft. One side window opposite the driver was removed and a camera was affixed there facing the driver. This gave the cameras the ability to view all the actors in the boat and the boat driver from the front and the side. When David was required behind the wheel, we set the boat up featuring him and the cameramen would shoot as quickly as possible and then fill in the scenes back at the studio.

All these people—about twenty-five in a small, thirty-foot yacht—with cameras, sound equipment, and other necessary filmmaking equipment, were loaded onto the boat. The boat began to take on water. I went to Jerry and told him there was too much weight on the boat. He did not question my judgment and only asked how many he could leave on the boat. I told him to have the technicians leave the boat in order of importance until I was satisfied, and he did so. My criterion for this decision was until the boat came up above the scuppers (water line).

John Wayne's yacht, the *Wild Goose*, was a sister ship to Jacques Cousteau's *Calypso*. Jacques Cousteau made an offer through my company, the Yacht Company Limited, for a small ship, about three hundred feet, to service a fleet of boats designed to lure tuna into an opening in the hull and to flash freeze them. The object was to deliver high-quality tuna to Japan in the very freshest condition and in the minimum time. The sea trail was off Athens, Greece, from the port of Piraeus. The ship failed its trial as it took a mile to stop, but I spent a wonderful week in Greece. I spent time in the port city of Piraeus. The largest yachts there were from the Middle East, primarily Saudi Arabia.

During my stay, the Russians were courting Greece, and a battleship and a destroyer were on display for the Greek citizens. I joined the line of tourists and was allowed aboard. On the rear of the destroyer was a Russian navy band. The band members looked to be about sixteen years of age. There was a large hopper, like a small plastic swimming pool, filled with books, mostly by Lenin and free to the locals. I took my share. I traveled the country, including Olympia, home of the Olympics. It is a beautiful country. While in Greece I toured the local Greek islands such as Corfu. Ouzo, Metaxas 5X, and Retsina were added to my list of drinks. It was 1976. I was forty-one. My daughter Mariah was born.

CHAPTER 23

Back in California, I became a dealer for Cal Yachts, a sailboat line, and became their top dealer in the United States. I imported yachts from Japan, Hong Kong, and Taiwan. I traveled to the Orient frequently. I became comfortable in foreign countries. I met many wealthy men and as a successful broker developed an ease around wealth.

I was drinking constantly and continued to gradually lose my sense of morality.* Whenever I had a money crunch, I would cut corners, always intending to repay the money before it could be missed. Before my sobriety, when I considered a deal, I considered all aspects of the deal, not just the legal ones. This interesting period illustrated my mental morality and the extent to which I would go to "hit a home run" rather than plod day to day.

*Loss of Morality, a Consequence of Alcoholism

An Example

Espirito Santo

A client told me of a World War II veteran who had been stationed with a pal in the South Pacific in the US Air Force's southernmost base, the New Hebrides Island grouping, specifically Espirito Santo. This air force sergeant and his pal were on Espirito Santo when the war ended. The base had Caterpillar tractors, road graders, generators, and all the equipment necessary to develop and operate an airbase. The disabled aircraft, at the end of the war, were simply pushed into the ocean. I was able to see some aircraft past the surf line. The heavy equipment, bulldozers, graders, etc., was in a deep covered pit dug to preserve the equipment. The "Cats" were never returned to the United States as they were operated by cable rather than hydraulics and were deemed not worth the cost.

During World War II, radio equipment was wired with silver wire as silver oxidizes very slowly and was therefore very efficient and long-lasting in radios. The base was equipped with a large supply of silver, perhaps several hundred pounds, and the two radiomen decided to hide it when the war ended as they believed it would not be missed. Therefore, they took 4 x 8 plywood sheets and built two boxes of sixty-four cubic feet each. The silver was wrapped in cosmaline and plastic, sealed well, and buried.

The airmen, after the war, were afraid to tell what they had done and additionally had no way to retrieve the silver. One evening, in a tavern in Boston and under the influence, the surviving airman told someone the story of the theft. How the story got to San Diego I am not certain, but someone in San Diego learned of the hidden silver. Rather than assume the story was true, they traveled to Boston and had the old sergeant hypnotized. They became convinced the story was true.

My reputation for taking chances and having access to large yachts brought this "deal" to me as they could not decide how to smuggle the silver into the United States. I had the "perfect" solution: deliver a sailboat to the New Hebrides without a lead keel from my factory in Taipei, Taiwan. These yachts normally had lead keels of the appropriate weight of the silver to be substituted. A thin layer of lead could be poured over the silver, and we were confident we could return to San Diego with the silver and market it privately and tax free. You must recall that when I considered a situation, I did not consider any possibility of trouble due to illegality.

I therefore flew to the New Hebrides with a stop in Fiji, where I hired a taxi to show me the sights. The driver took me to where the islanders were preparing a local drug, kava, in the jungle. Kava users could be easily identified as the drug turned the islanders' teeth black and put them into a stupor. I did not try it. One more note about Fiji that may be of interest: Fiji has imported men and women from India in the past and they have slowly taken over commerce from the laid-back Fijians to every one's satisfaction.

My flight from Fiji to Espirito Santo was in a small twin-engine plane that transported both passengers and freight. Passenger seats were removed when the plane was carrying freight. My flight was scheduled for later in the day, but the pilot of a flight for freight only offered me a seat up front with him and I accepted with alacrity. I could not resist telling him of my flight training, and when we were in the air, he said the plane was mine. I flew the balance of the way to the New Hebrides as he filled in his form 1. It was my first experience in a multi-engine aircraft.

Espirito Santo had a "condominium government," half French and half English. The very modest capitol building had a clear separation right down the middle with an English flag over one side and a French flag over the other. My lodging was a comfortable room with live geckos on the walls and a bathroom down the hall.

I soon hired islanders with a backhoe. I had brought a metal detector. The map I had indicated the site of the buried silver, which was in a grove of banyan trees. A banyan tree starts its life as a strangling fig growing on another tree, eventually completely enveloping it and dropping roots down from branches that become trunks. Banyans can take over an area. Where there may have been a single banyan tree during World War II, there was now a multitude of trunks covering a large area. This was true over the map site. Also, the mineral content of the soil made it nearly impossible to get good readings with metal detectors. Eventually we dug up a large area with no results. It seemed possible someone had beaten us to the silver. Finally, I abandoned the effort and returned to San Diego. My flight was delayed for two days as natives in traditional dress lined themselves across the runway in some sort of defiant act against the local government. This was about 1980. I was forty-five.

CHAPTER 24

TAIWAN AND CHINA

Back in San Diego, having sold the old company, I started a new company, Royal Ensign Yachts. I attracted wealthy men who shared my spirit of adventure. One of my new partners owned auto parts stores, another owned song rights in Hollywood, and another had a factory making recreational vehicles. We flew together to Taiwan with several objectives: to purchase yachts for two of the partners, to get prices for seat belts for the RV company, and to obtain auto parts. The man involved with song rights, already quite wealthy, was there for adventure.

One of these new partners was experienced in traveling to Taipei. He had bought many products for his auto stores and knew how to operate at that level in Taipei. The flights to the Orient in those days were not nonstop—we stopped in Tokyo, for example—and were long. It was his habit to go to a Chinese "spa" for a treatment after landing. The treatment was to invigorate us after the long flight.

The Chinese "spa" was quite an experience. First we took a long hot soapy bath, then we were rubbed down with a folded wash rag so briskly that the masseuse rubbed the old epidermis off and piled it on our chest. The pile grew to several inches high. Caucasians are considered dirty with all their old skin. The next treatment was another long, hot, soapy bath, then back and forth into pools of very cold water then again into hot water. Next came a shave and a manicure and a pedicure using an X-ACTO knife. The manicurists were amazingly skillful and did each finger and toe with amazing speed. Next was a thorough massage, somewhat rough and not at all sensual. Then the masseuse walked on your back—you could hear and feel your bones cracking, but not at all unpleasantly. The total result was interesting and invigorating.

Our hotel was comfortable but not fancy. Our next project was to meet with companies to obtain prices for the seat belts; this was done in the evening from our hotel room. Representatives arrived that same evening. By morning, the representatives, usually the "factory" owners, called on us with actual product and prices. We visited the selected vendor and found his factory was not large and modern but very shabby and nondescript. Nevertheless, my partner had always been satisfied with this vendor's price and quality and remained so over the next years.

Business, as in the imported yacht business, was conducted with letters of credit. We all had separate hotel rooms, and the other men availed themselves of the local women of the night. Each floor had a woman in charge of that floor; the "ladies" checked in with this person and apparently relied on her to alert the hotel if there was any problem and probably to pay the hotel's share. This was one of the only vices in which I did not participate.

We were all having drinks in the hotel room of the man from Hollywood. On his request, I opened his dresser drawer in order to get money to pay for room service, and it was filled with New Taiwanese dollars. I hardly had to pay for a thing. A memorable dinner was held at a famous local restaurant featuring geishas. A geisha was seated on a small stool behind but near each of us. The *mama-san* changed the geishas if she sensed one of us seemed not to be pleased with our geisha. I was the only one shy about having a geisha, and the *mama-san* kept changing my geisha as I seemed not to respond properly to the one assigned to me. Finally, I was told the next geisha had never been sent back. The new geisha was stunning, and I showed proper appreciation and avoided a problem. The geishas were available, and the others took their geishas with them. The dinner itself was memorable and we were almost not allowed to use our own utensils as the geishas fed us with chopsticks. It was an exceptional experience.

More often. I traveled alone to purchase yachts. The factory owners and favored executives enjoyed entertaining the buyers. Their motivation was to entertain themselves as it was tax deductible. I was taken to dance halls, where they purchased dance tickets to use to dance with the ladies employed there. I was a bit too shy for this form of entertainment and was generally ignored as the men got more and more inebriated. The dancing was not my form of behavior, but the Chinese beer was. Marlboro cigarettes were the most popular brand in Taipei but were more expensive than the local brand. The local brand, its name translated into English, was called Long Life.

Another evening, after a large purchase of yachts, I qualified for their ultimate form of entertainment. During World War II, Taiwan was named Formosa and under Japanese control. Officers were sent to Formosa for rest and recreation in a beautiful area dedicated especially for that purpose. That resort area still existed. The brothels, hotels, and restaurants were in an area near Taipei in the mountains. I was taken there and "honored" with an ultimate dinner. This dinner was on a table for four of us: the president, his top two executives, and me. The table featured a small hole in the center. The purpose of the hole, I was to discover, was for their prime delicacy, the head of a monkey with its brain exposed. I was not able or inclined to participate, but their enjoyment was apparent.

Next, I was taken to a club of sorts where we joined a group of men around several large, round tables, where the only activity was drinking a savage alcoholic drink, clear and exceptionally strong, washed down with beer. Each man around the table, when it became his turn, would offer a toast, mostly in Chinese. I barely recall making one when it became my turn. Then the toast would be made from a shot glass. The drink was a strong Chinese liquor called Baijio. The person proposing the toast would shout "*Ganbei*," which indicates you are to drink the liquor in one swallow. I cannot remember the number of toasts, and I do not recall the balance of the evening.

CHAPTER 25

On another trip to Taiwan, my wife, Ginny, and my sales manager, Dusty Rhodes, traveled with me. As we arrived, we noted a cultural difference in the hotel elevator; on the wall was a picture of a "typical" American breakfast in the view of the hotel's "American" restaurant. It was a picture of two fried eggs and a wiener sitting starkly on a bone white plate: not at all appetizing. I came to learn this was how Chinese assumed sausage and eggs looked.

Ginny refused to eat there and instead chose to go to the Chinese-only restaurant there at the hotel. At this restaurant no one spoke English and the panicked staff called the hotel manager. He arrived and was immediately taken with Ginny. He ordered dinner for us and was with us for every meal thereafter. One evening we had fish served whole—head, skin, and all. It was quite delicious. The custom of the upper class was to eat only the top side, although the manager confided the custom was not observed in private.

I took Ginny and Dusty with me to the CT Chen boat factory to order yachts, which was my reason for the trip. While at the factory we were surrounded by the factory owners, the factory managers, and all those with a part in construction and cost. We were ordering several million dollars' worth of yachts and it was an important occasion for the company. During the meeting, we were served tea in glasses, warm, not hot, with a cover on the glass, and beer if we chose.

After several hours of tea and beer, Ginny, the only female, found she needed a restroom and asked for directions. The Chinese were so involved they simply waved their hands at what seemed to Ginny to be the stairs. She went up the stairs searching for the facilities and found herself in a large garden on the roof of the factory. It was a large vegetable garden including enclosures for pigeons. She could find no restroom and was gone a long time. Suddenly it occurred to the men that the wife of the customer was missing. A huge search ensued. Ginny was found in the garden and a woman worker took her to the "ladies' room": an open shack with multiple holes in the ground, visible from the road and not at all private.

As we were leaving the factory, we observed an open truck driving away full of grown pigs. They were strangely all sitting on their haunches facing forward with looks of fatalism. We learned most of the factory workers lived on the premises and each raised a pig in their quarters until it was grown; the pigs considered themselves part of the family only to be sent off to slaughter.

Back in the city, in the evening, we visited the night market. In downtown Taipei, the streets are closed for autos in the evening in a large area and filled with stalls selling nearly any product or service wanted or needed. One of the most interesting sights was the acupuncture stalls, chairs placed on the street with people sitting with needles sticking out of them. The men were usually shirtless and covered with needles.

Another strange sight was people walking along eating snakes. We followed and found the source: a stall with a glass container full of small live snakes, about eighteen inches long, was located next to a pot full of hot boiling oil. The customer would select a snake and the vendor would drop it live into the oil. Cooked, it would take its last alive shape and the customer would walk down the street with the crooked snake in his hand eating it as if were a corn dog.

We also visited a department store; perhaps Ginny needed lingerie. Near the bra section, the young female Taiwanese shopkeepers were tittering and touching Ginny's breasts. Why we were not sure, perhaps curiosity about a Caucasian woman. In the same store, in a machine like a popcorn machine, were fried chicken legs for sale. These were from the knee joint down.

CHAPTER 26

HONG KONG AND CHINA

On the way back to San Diego, we stopped in Hong Kong. Hong Kong, as you are no doubt aware, is a major world city with a population of more than 7 million, and its skyscrapers rival those in most cities in the world. At that time a British colony, Hong Kong is now part of China.

Mainland China was previously separated from Hong Kong by the "New Territory," apparently neither China nor Hong Kong. We took a train, not very modern, across the New Territory and visited mainland China. On the way, we observed a moderate-sized hill with a white masonry circular fenced area of about one hundred yards in diameter. It was filled with gravestones. We learned that because of space limitations, people cannot stay buried for more than one year. Thereafter their bones are interred and thrown in a "bone yard" on the property.

The village past the New Territory was very primitive. On arrival one of the tourists took a Polaroid picture of curious locals and motioned for them to watch it develop. When the picture began to appear, it frightened them so much they ran away.

Young soldiers patrolled the area. They wore military green uniforms and carried rifles. We were told not to take a picture of the soldiers; we asked why. "Because they will shoot you," we were told. The soldiers looked to be about fifteen and their shoes appeared to be green tennis shoes with separations for toes. We also visited a local shrine in the middle of a lake; it was quite beautiful in the Chinese style. I left my bag with my passport there. It was quite a chore retrieving it, but I was able to do so. Being without a passport in mainland China is not recommended.

One favorite evening, we went by boat to Victoria Island, which is just across the bay from the city of Hong Kong, and had a Chinese dinner at the world-famous Jumbo floating restaurant. Our meal was excellent. After the meal, we were taken around the little bay, which was full of liveaboard sampans and other small liveaboard boats full of children and adults begging. Tourists would pitch money down to them and they would catch the money no matter how poorly thrown even if it meant jumping into the bay.

Cheoy Lee Yachts was one of my boat factories in Hong Kong. I was amazed to see its location on the side of a steep hill hundreds of feet up. Cheoy Lee yachts are well known for their quality and beauty. That they came out of that factory was amazing to me. Of course, it was probably not the only factory. Local Chinese boats such as sampans have an exaggerated keel, very deep at the stern. I was soon to learn why. They are constructed in an area on a steep bank on the bay's edge. To keep the hull level during construction, the keel in the stern is very deep. The boat is then pushed into the water.

CHAPTER 27

Back in San Diego in 1983, two wealthy gay men purchased a yacht from me and ordered it completely remodeled. The cost grew out of their range and they asked me to sink it for the insurance. Oddly, no one seemed to hesitate to ask me to do something illegal; given the alcoholic person I had become, one without good morality, I agreed without curiosity. I include these instances of my declining character in order to introduce the reader to the erosion of morality of those with the disease of alcoholism.

Several of us took the yacht into Mexican waters and on the way lost power and radio. What was to become a purposeful sinking became an accident. Over several hours we drifted toward a Mexican shore. Finally, although dark, we could see the shore, and it was not friendly. We were midway between Tijuana and Rosarita in Baja California. The shore was solid rocky cliffs, and into the surf we drifted. One of the waves turned the boat over violently and dumped us all into the water. I could hear the others screaming. I hit the rocks and found a small perch in the cliff's edge. Both of the other passengers were fortunate to be beached on a small sandy area nearby. I returned to the scene of the crash the next day and found the boat had been smashed into tiny pieces; the largest I saw was less than two feet long. I could not see the engines and transmissions. They must have been in deeper water.

We waved a passing car down and got back to San Diego. We were saved from wrecking the yacht illegally by sheer chance. One of my passengers asked not to be mentioned as a passenger on the Coast Guard report. He was not allowed to be in Mexico because of a previous drug arrest. These were my fellows. That same guy was later drinking in a bar in San Diego and loudly told friends about the experience. A couple in the next booth heard the conversation and turned us in to the police and the insurance company, who then refused the claim.

CHAPTER 28

PRISON AND ITS EFFECTS

As the incident became an accident, I was not charged with insurance fraud, but with making a false statement on the Coast Guard report, although they were aware of the greater crime. I spent fifty-nine days in federal prison, where I was known as the Old Man. I also had a five-year probation period.

I was in good company at the Federal Metropolitan Correctional Institute (MCI) in San Diego. J. David Dominelli was a cellmate. His Ponzi scheme cost San Diego investors $80,000,000. Another noteworthy prisoner was a Las Vegas mafioso who owned a well-known casino; the inmates treated him like royalty. There was a definite hierarchical system.

My time in prison was interesting, although boring at the same time. I worked in the library. Once a week we were taken to the rooftop exercise area for the prisoners. Each evening, after dinner, a line formed outside of my cell of people looking for "business" advice. The method of payment was quarters, cigarettes, and candy. Such was my reputation. Each cell had its own window, but it was so narrow you could not get out of it.

CHAPTER 29

When my sentence was up, I gave my little radio to a young Mexican man in prison for shooting up a courtroom in Los Angeles where his father was on trial. Shortly after he was released, he called me and asked if I needed anyone killed as repayment of the favor. This was May 1985. I was forty-nine.

I bought a beer on my release from prison. I had learned nothing about a disease of which I was not aware. I went back into the yacht business with a friend who owned a major brokerage located in the Marriot Hotels harbor marina. I was soon again prospering. While there, I participated in the sale of a large yacht to Jerry Lewis, who lived on the yacht at the marina. I gained respect for Jerry Lewis as I found his income from his widely known annual telethon was a total donation to the March of Dimes charity.

One of the inmates who had given me a quarter for "business" advice while we were in prison was released after me. He soon after stole a large Caterpillar road grader and sent it to me from up north in Washington or Oregon to sell. He knew I was acquainted with the family who owned the Caterpillar dealership. Luckily, my morality—or was it fear?—was returning. I was not willing to be involved. This was to prove fortunate. Later, I answered the doorbell to find a stern FBI agent at my door. He sat me down on my couch. Ginny was there with me. He opened his briefcase, looked at some papers, and began asking questions. Very fortunately, I chose to answer truthfully, and after a lengthy period, he closed his briefcase and informed Ginny and me that if I had not been truthful on any question, he would have returned me to prison to serve the balance of my probation period, nearly five years. My probation was for five years, during which time the FBI became aware I was on probation and participated in my probation. As a result, I have an FBI number. The agent overseeing my parole was Japanese. I came to admire his ethics, and he was instrumental in my becoming a better citizen.

One day, I was called in to be interviewed as the main element of a sting in Europe. It involved the sale of nuclear materiel about which I had been approached; I notified the FBI as a result of my relationship with my agent, a fortunate thing. The case was cleared before I had to participate. My reviews were becoming mixed.

CHAPTER 30

OTHER ENDEAVORS

During this time, I was hired as the executive vice president of an oil and gas company based in Southern California, the president of which was a founding member of the Harlem Globetrotters. I will not use his name. I was probably selected to raise money for the corporation as this was becoming my primary skill. It was a "penny stock" company. With some of my old "pals" I began raising cash for the company. I discovered the company owned mining claims in the California desert south of Las Vegas. This is near a rare-earth mine on the California–Nevada border, which is important today as rare earths are vital to aerospace and high-tech companies.

An acquaintance, Bill N., was in the mining business, and I hired his company to evaluate the properties. He did so. Later, he approached me and asked for help in collecting his fee. I was unsuccessful. While still in the employ of the oil company, I went to the property, selected some ore with Bill's guidance, crushed the ore, treated it with the methods he provided, put it in a small crucible then into an oven, and made the most amazing gold ball about the size of the head of a match. It was beautiful, the gold ball shone, and even Bill was amazed. I showed it to the president of the oil company, who had friends at Princeton University. He and I flew to New York City, took a hotel on Central Park, hired a limousine, and drove to Princeton University, where I made a presentation to a group of engineers. My presentation was well received by the engineers, but unsuccessful as the investment needed was beyond their ability. Nevertheless, the trip was interesting and constructive.

A NEW CONCEPT

Bill N., unable to collect his fee, felt he had no longer an obligation to the oil company. He came to San Diego and told me the result of the evaluation. He told me the claims owned by the company were hard rock claims abandoned during World War II. There were many of these claims, mostly covered with railroad ties and soil. We examined several, and below they were in the same good condition as when the claim owners had abandoned them.

Although the values of the claims were high, extraction would be expensive. During the evaluation, Bill checked an adjacent site, a caldera formed when the magma emptied from a volcano. The base of the caldera, he felt, would have gold from erosion; through assays he found the values very acceptable. The values were lower, but the lesser cost of extraction would make it very viable. Later we made a deal to capitalize a mining company. I left the oil company.

CHAPTER 31

I had three other interesting businesses in this time period: a yacht customer from Phoenix was originally from Pennsylvania, near Punxsutawney, the little town famous for Groundhog Day. He was a customer for a large sailboat, and we became friends. His business was photograph development. He had developed a business supplying development chemicals to photo shops whereby they made their own developing solutions. There was an enormous savings involved and great potential. Unfortunately, those businesses became dinosaurs with the advent of digital photography.

He and I then switched to coal mining; he had acreage in Pennsylvania rich in coal, but never had the capital to develop the property. I raised enough capital to evaluate the property. We did core drillings and discovered a vein several feet thick with financial potential. This vein would require surface mining, though, and the expenditure and permitting required rendered the project unviable.

Next I purchased, with a partner, a small long-distance telephone company located in the Los Angeles area. We expanded into San Diego and were able to get the contract for wiring, for telephone service, the newest and largest "skyscraper" in San Diego. The America's Cup was being held in San Diego, and this was a successful coup. I sold my interest and moved into the heavyweight fight arena. My only involvement in the boxing business was with a Larry Holmes fight.

CHAPTER 32

PROMOTING A WORLD HEAVYWEIGHT FIGHT

Larry Holmes was a world champion heavyweight fighter. He won sixty-nine fights, and was one of only five men to defeat Mohammed Ali. Larry was involved with some litigation, I do not recall what, and was temporarily without an agent. We learned of the opportunity to promote the fight. I traveled to Los Angeles with a partner and met Larry and his entourage at his suite at the Beverly Hilton. The entourage was quite large, perhaps ten, mostly men, all black. I was the only white guy there as my partner was also black.

We just missed Sylvester Stallone; he was there just before us and had made an offer to promote the fight. He left his contract there and we altered it to make our offer. We were chosen. To celebrate, Larry ordered twenty hamburgers and bottles of Blue Nun wine. I could not imagine why he selected us to promote the fight. I was later to learn the reason: Larry insisted on having the fight in his hometown, which was an extremely poor venue for a heavyweight fight.

As I began my attempts to sell the fight, calling ESPN and other television companies specializing in sports, I was having great difficulty making a deal due to Larry's restrictions. Then Don King came on the scene and we began to get death threats. We contacted Larry, and he said that although he hated Don King, he was being forced to join him to promote the fight. Larry's mother, who was a great lady, told Larry, "Larry you give those white boys their money back [$25,000]."

We had also begun getting threats in San Diego. The local boxing promoter, whose name I cannot use, had strongly suggested we listen to Don King. As an aside, we had an African American maid at the time, and she and Larry talked frequently. I do not know if this in any way influenced the proceedings; however, she immediately thereafter left our employ. Hmm.

CHAPTER 33

THE NORMANDY INVASION TOUR TO PARIS

In the spring of 1984, the idea of taking a group to Paris to celebrate the anniversary of the invasion of Normandy in northern France was conceived. I had previously been to Paris to buy and import Mercedes automobiles, a moderately successful venture. During this visit, I met an attorney from New York, whom I shall call Robert. We shared a suite while in Paris.

Back in San Diego, we advertised for a tour of the site of the Normandy invasion and therefore concentrated on veterans and the American Legion. We planned the trip to coincide with the fortieth anniversary of D-Day, June 6, 1984.

While in Paris I had joined the American Legion, Post Number One, established in Paris after World War II; it was a wonderful social and drinking club for expatriates. We therefore visited American Legion Posts and we were able to interest a group of more than fifty couples. I chartered a bus to take us to Los Angeles, and a DC-10 to fly us from Los Angeles to Amsterdam. In Amsterdam, I chartered a bus to Paris, arriving in the evening. This was in 1984. I was forty-nine years old.

We unloaded at the American Legion Post in Paris, and my partner was not to be found; he was to have arranged the hotels. I handled the problem by getting drunk. Finally, my partner showed up and we got everyone in their hotels. The group was angry enough that they called a meeting the next morning that I would rather forget. However, on balance the trip was successful. I brought my family: Ginny, Rhett, Cindy, Nathan, and Mariah. It was a rare opportunity for the family to see Paris, the Eiffel Tower, the Louvre, the Palace at Versailles, and more. Nathan spent his birthday on the Eiffel Tower on September 9, 1984.

CHAPTER 34

THE ARMS BUSINESS

While in Paris at an earlier time, I stayed in a hotel that housed a consultant team from Zimbabwe; we became friendly with many of them. The Russians at that time were "courting" Zimbabwe, and they were often together in a meeting room in the basement of the hotel. The meeting room was downstairs near the restrooms, and when we needed to visit the restroom during these meetings, Russian escorts accompanied us. They looked exactly like the Russians depicted in comics—wearing dark suits and stocky. We were invited to visit their government offices in Harare, Zimbabwe. My newest business partner, a retired Marine colonel, made the trip for our group. Meeting and having long talks with the ambassador and his subordinates was my introduction into the arms business.

The arms business was a good fit for me, as truthfulness and morality were subjects about which I was not yet totally conversant. As such, I spent much of my time over the next few years in France, especially Paris, in Germany, and across Europe. I clearly remember clandestine meetings on roof decks overlooking Paris and the Eiffel Tower. Many meetings were held in the marbled halls of the George Cinq [George V] Hotel in Paris, Hitler's headquarters during Germany's occupation during World War II. Other meetings took place in the south of France on the Rivera. Many other meetings occurred across Europe and the Middle East.

As I gazed down the halls of the George Cinq, among the many coffee tables and comfortable chairs I could see groups of men studying catalogs of guns, tanks, uniforms, and other accouterments of war. I did so also with customers buying uniforms, guns, etc., usually for African nations. It is a quite different world. Third world countries have a layer of men (and perhaps women, although I never dealt with a woman) who take a percentage of the cost of these materials and equipment. They are allowed to do so due to their nobility or political importance.

One evening, I was at a famous Paris hotel. Jimmy Carter had stayed there while on a government trip to Paris. I was there with my attorney from New York, now a member of my arms sales team, and we had a prized table in the discothèque. As the disco became crowded, a trio of young men from Bahrain sent a waiter over to ask if they could join our table. We said yes and learned the men, in their thirties, were in fact Bahrain princes.

We were not able to spend a penny from then on and found they were very curious about Americans. One of the young men asked if he had made a fair purchase on his sport coat. He said he only paid $1,200 for it. The evening was quite interesting, and at the end of the night, the young men invited us up to their suite to continue the party. I declined, but my friend accepted. They arranged for a private room for him at the end of the festivities. The next day he told me they had asked if he would like company and he had agreed it would be nice. They then asked if he preferred a young woman or a young man: a woman, he said.

On another occasion, I flew to Dusseldorf, Germany, to meet with a German general who had a customer with a use permit from an African country that enabled that country to purchase American C-130s aircraft, commonly called Hercules. The price to be paid to him for the transaction was $1 million, to be paid as per instructions given in the letter of credit. Letters of credit are used in these transactions. They are paid only after the completion of all details of the contract.

Hercules aircraft are popular in Africa due to their ability to land on short, primitive runways, their long range, and their ability to carry large payloads. The US government requires a use permit from the country to which the aircraft are sold. These permits were used by those in power to accumulate wealth without it becoming common knowledge. These men had the power to get the permits from, for example, another powerful man from, usually in my experience, an African nation. The arrangement between them was not discussed. They would then use this permit to allow the sale of aircraft, tanks, uniforms, arms, or other such items to their country. The terms of the sale would include their fee.

Another interesting sale involved an order for a number of tanks delivered to the Middle East. A conflict was occurring at that time, and the ship delivering the tanks was not allowed to dock. The letter of credit expired before delivery could be accomplished, and the sale was never completed, at least by me—my first big "non-deal." The commission would have been more than $1 million, shared with my team, of course.

I came to realize the US government allowed the sale of US military surplus, such as the Hercules, only if the sale achieved a balance among the warring or competing countries. If the sale resulted in an embarrassment to the US government, the government would prosecute those involved in the sale. This knowledge caused me to leave the arms trade. This was about 1985. I would soon turn fifty years old.

CHAPTER 35

SHADOW VALLEY MINING COMPANY

Back in San Diego, I was asked to capitalize the Shadow Valley Mining Company. The Shadow Valley Mining Company was to become a gold and platinum group mining company. Shadow Valley is located just west of Highway 15 in California just before the Nevada state line. Las Vegas is seventy-five miles further north.

My new partners, who had done the evaluation on the oil and gas company property, had decided to claim the area around the claims they had evaluated. Their claims covered twenty-two sections. A section is one square mile, 640 acres, an area of more than 14,000 acres. I raised the initial necessary capitol, $100,000, and became one of five equal partners. My title was executive vice president. I was second in command, although I knew nothing about mining. But I had a bit of business and fundraising experience. Much more about the Shadow Mining Company will follow later.

CHAPTER 36

THE END OF MY DRINKING

All this time, my drinking was getting progressively worse. One evening, my son, age sixteen, came home under the influence of methamphetamines, or crystal, as it was called. I recognized he was an addict but still did not realize I was an alcoholic. I struck him, probably several times, and bloodied him up just as Ginny came into the room. She suddenly realized our drinking, especially mine, was no longer within any bounds of acceptability. She went into a room alone and began praying to the God of her youth and had a spiritual experience not unlike that Bill Wilson, the cofounder of AA, had experienced. A spiritual experience of this type was not to be a part of my journey.

The next day, Ginny went to an Al-Anon meeting. Al-Anon is a fellowship of men and women whose lives have been affected by the compulsive drinking of a family member or friend. There she learned she also met the requirement to join AA, a fellowship of men and women who share their experiences, strength, and hope with each other in hope they may solve their common problem (alcoholism) and help others to recover from it.

Ginny started attending AA meetings and immediately began to feel at peace. She suggested we go to an AA meeting together. My behavior (usually financial) was such that I was often in trouble with her, so I agreed to attend only to placate her. I often agreed with Ginny to get out of whatever problem I was currently experiencing. It was my intention to go to AA with here only if it would get her over this idea of us no longer drinking. This was January 6, 1986. I was fifty.

During the very first meeting we attended together, a man announced a program just formed called Couples in Recovery. These Couples in Recovery meetings were begun by Dr. Paul Ohliger and his wife, Max, famous in AA as the author of "Doctor, Alcoholic, Addict," a chapter in the AA book. His famous work was on the subject of acceptance.

We went to the second meeting ever held in San Diego and have continued to attend for more than thirty-five years now. We attended a Couples in Recovery workshop on Big Bear Mountain just east of Los Angeles and met Dr. Paul. At a private meeting with Dr. Paul, Ginny told him she was having trouble with the concept of acceptance. He replied that *acceptance does not mean approval.*

We would later learn the importance of that concept,

A secret of sobriety

At that first meeting, I met a man who became my AA sponsor. A sponsor is a person who teaches you the AA program and supports your recovery. Sponsorship is a tradition in AA. It is suggested that men have male sponsors and women have female sponsors.

In AA, the recovery process is called "doing the steps," which are the suggestions for attaining sobriety and remaining sober. My new sponsor immediately took me to an all-men's meeting of about one hundred men with a lot of years of sobriety among them. All this was very strange to me as I do not recall knowing anything about AA. I did not consider myself an alcoholic, especially as I did not know about or understand alcoholism. I was vaguely aware my drinking was causing problems in my life without an understanding of or curiosity as to why.

In the beginning of going to meetings, I was able to act as if I was an alcoholic in order to fit in. I have come to understand this is what is known as "people pleasing." This was a long-time behavior of mine. Strangely, I began to feel quite comfortable in the meetings and did not drink.

A secret of sobriety

In the beginning, I was anxious to be accepted and liked, again, a people pleaser. I did read the AA book several times in the first weeks. Later I realized I read the book at a very shallow level. Slowly, however, I began to enjoy the program without understanding or being curious about its dynamics. Acting "as if" was a fortunate first step for my recovery. I did not yet understand or believe AA could work, *but I began to believe those in AA believed.* This was sufficient for me.

CHAPTER 37

SOMETHING ABOUT ALCOHOLICS ANONYMOUS

As I have indicated, I was ignorant of the disease of alcoholism and about AA. My natural curiosity required I become informed. Here is the beginning of what I was to learn. The AA program, again, requires participants to "do the steps." These steps have been winnowed from AA's beginnings.

1. We admitted we were powerless over alcohol—that our lives had become unmanageable.

2. Came to believe that *a power greater than ourselves* could restore us to sanity.

3. Decided to turn our will and our lives over to the care of God *as we understood Him.*

4. Made a searching and moral inventory of ourselves.

5. Admitted to God, to ourselves, and to another human being the exact nature of our wrongs.

6. Were entirely ready to have God remove all these defects of character.

7. Humbly asked Him to remove our shortcomings.

8. Made a list of all persons we had harmed and became willing to make amends to them all.

9. Made direct amends to such people whenever possible, except when to do so would injure them or others.

10. Continued to take personal inventory and when we were wrong promptly admitted it.

11. Sought through prayer and meditation to improve our conscious contact with God *as we understood Him*, praying only for knowledge of His will for us and the power to carry that out.

12. Having had a spiritual awakening as the result of these steps, we tried to carry this message to alcoholics, and to practice these principles in all our affairs.

CHAPTER 38

ALCOHOLICS ANONYMOUS AS IT APPLIED TO ME

LEARNING THE STEPS

Having had no spiritual awakening when first I read these steps, they made no impression on my attitude concerning drinking or my understanding of the steps. Perhaps they did not apply to me but were useful to others. These were some of my earlier thoughts. They also express my earliest experiences in AA and some of my progress, but also my much later understanding of the steps. Remember, this is merely my experience.

Step 1. We admitted we were powerless over alcohol—that our lives had become unmanageable. My experience: I did not comprehend the meaning of Step 1. What did it mean to be powerless over alcohol? My life unmanageable? I think not!

Step 2. Came to believe that a power greater than ourselves could return us to sanity.

A power greater than me—they were talking about God. I had given up on God a long time ago, and I was quite aggressive about it, teasing others, especially Ginny's brother and his wife, about their Christian beliefs.

Step 3. Decided to turn our will and our lives over to the care of God as we understand Him. You might guess my attitude. Here were my thoughts. Spirituality and what was termed "a power greater than ourselves"—what I came to call the "God Thing"—is a major stumbling block for many, if not most, in the AA program. We are told to turn our will and our lives "over to the care of a *power greater than ourselves*." This was far beyond my early ability.

Of course I quickly saw the subterfuge here: they were talking about God. Well yes, they were in the beginning. Alcoholics Anonymous nearly became a Christian program, as I was to discover. As a Christian program,

AA would have surely failed. Certainly it would not have the international appeal it has now. This was to become my understanding of the step much later.

Enough atheists and agnostics joined the program that Bill Wilson, the cofounder of AA, had to rewrite the AA book, the first drafts of which were written in 1939. The AA book in its original draft was heavily Christian. The argument was these drunks either did not believe in God or thought their past behavior would make them ineligible for the program. I too so believed.

The major dissenter was a man named Jim B. Twenty years later, he confessed he had moderated his original view. This was not unusual. Alcoholics Anonymous lets you have your own concept of God, and over the years, most participants have returned to the religion of their youth, found one acceptable, or came to understand a power greater than them directs the universe. Whom or what that power was would take many forms. Albert Einstein, an avowed atheist, wrote: "The deep emotional conviction of the presence of a superior reasoning power ... is revealed in the incomprehensible universe." This forms my idea of God.

Since no one has adequately explained how the desire for alcohol suddenly is gone when no other method has been successful, I had to keep an open mind, which was difficult. A quote by Herbert Spencer became hard to ignore for myself and others in the program. "There is a principle which is a bar against all information, which is proof against all argument and which cannot fail to keep a man in everlasting ignorance—that principle is 'contempt prior to investigation.'"

A secret of sobriety

I would later take that advice. Many have quarreled about religion who never practiced it. That also would apply to me. This was my own situation although I had had two spiritual occurrences in my life, one in my youth and another in my thirties. Both were of the Christian variety, involving a strong emotional experience that led me to the front of the church to the altar and to the preacher. In front of the congregation I expressed belief in God. I clearly recall these experiences. Nevertheless, subsequently I let my education tell me this kind of experience was some sort of psychological behavior or quirk.

Bill Wilson had the same thought after his emotional "white light" experience. His experience was so strong he decided to talk to a doctor experienced in such cases. That doctor, Dr. Silkworth, told him that indeed these experiences are rare but exist and have extraordinary results. I had no such experience. I was much too young in AA. Eventually I was to have a spiritual experience of the educational variety.

Many churches are embarrassed their own recovery programs are not successful in getting members sober. These churches usually will not allow AA in their facilities, choosing rather to design a system of their own. These systems are not as successful as AA—an understatement—and many of their participants eventually find their way into AA, often, perhaps, to the chagrin of their pastors. These pastors fail to see this might have been God's plan for their church.

In AA, we say, *"God brought us to AA and AA brought us to God."* We maintain AA is a spiritual rather than a religious program. We have been heard to say that religion is for people trying to stay out of hell, but spirituality is for those of us who have already been there. An apt expression.

A spiritual or Christian experience, one of the alter calls I just mentioned, brought about a three- or four-year period of not drinking for me and my wife. I said not drinking, not sobriety! A stress came later that started my drinking again. I had none of the tools I was to later find in AA to resist the urge. Ginny joined me. Alcoholics Anonymous was to come later.

Step 4. Made a searching and fearless moral inventory of ourselves. This step was of major difficulty for me. I was required to recount the behaviors I had engaged in during my drinking episodes and those I had harmed while doing so. This requirement puts your behavior on paper where it can no longer be ignored. I was simply not able to put any of my past on paper. Finally, after three years, my sponsor lost patience with me and told me to find a "step study."

A "step study" is, like the name implies, a meeting that studies the steps of the AA program. After a week, my sponsor asked me if I had found a step study. I answered there were none in the neighborhood. He lost his temper with me and told me to start one. He had essentially fired me.

Still, anxious to please and with the assistance of the Thursday Night Men's Meeting of Point Loma, I started a meeting. It became the Thursday Night Men's Step Study. This was in 1989. The meeting is now thirty-three years old as of this writing. I was fifty-three. The step study not only helped me, but it has also helped hundreds of others. Incredibly, I have managed some humility. *It was a start.*

Step 5. Admitted to God, to ourselves, and to another human being the exact nature of our wrongs. To admit to a God I did not yet understand, to another human being, and especially to myself "the exact nature of my wrongs" would require tools I did not yet have. Admitting to God I could handle. He was as yet impersonal. To admit to myself brought strong denial, and I did not yet have the tools to admit to another human being.

Step 6. Were entirely ready to have God remove all these defects of character. Again, I had no tools with which to prepare myself to allow an unknown God to remove my defects of character, which were not yet acknowledged. This was beyond my early ability.

Step 7. Humbly asked Him to remove our shortcomings. To humbly ask a yet to be acknowledged God for anything was not yet possible.

Step 8. Made a list of all persons we had harmed and became willing to make amends to them all. Making a list of those I had harmed proved difficult. Much of the harm done took place while I was under the influence, and it is therefore difficult to remember incidents in detail.

Step 9. Made direct amends to such people whenever possible, except when to do so would injure them or others. This means to apologize; I could not do that, nor did I think I should. They should make amends to me, some of them, I thought. This was my attitude in the beginning.

Step 10. Continued to take personal inventory, and when we were wrong, promptly admitted it. This was not an early behavior. Later Step 10 became important to my recovery.

Step 11. Sought through prayer and meditation to improve our constant contact with God, as we understood Him, praying only for knowledge of His will for us and the power to carry that out. This was not a part of my early program, but today it is a large part of it. Ginny and I spend well over an hour each day enjoying over twenty-one books of the day-at-a-time variety. It is the most important part of our day.

Step 12. Having had a spiritual awakening as a result of these steps, we tried to carry this message to other alcoholics, and to practice these principles in all our affairs. This was to become enormously important in my program as it developed, but it was impossible with the shallowness of my early program.

A Recap

This is a glimpse of where I was early in my participation in AA. Confused but learning, I was continuing in the program. Steps, 10, 11, and 12 involve daily inventory, prayer, and meditation, and describe a spiritual experience I had not (yet?) had. A spiritual experience of the educational variety was to come.

Eleven years later, in 1946, AA decided it needed a "manual" of explanation. Many things had occurred in those first eleven years that needed attention and clarification. For this reason, *The Twelve and Twelve* was written. It presents an explicit view of the principles by which AA members recover and by which the society functions. The full name is *The Twelve Steps and the Twelve Traditions*.

You have been exposed to the Twelve Steps. The Twelve Traditions apply to the life of the fellowship itself. They outline the means by which AA maintains its unity and relates itself to the world around it, the way it lives and grows. The Twelve Traditions are:

1. Our common welfare should come first; personal recovery depends upon AA unity.

2. For our group purpose there is but one ultimate authority—a loving God as He may express Himself in our group conscience. Our leaders are but trusted servants; they do not govern.

3. The only requirement for AA membership is a desire to stop drinking.

4. Each group should be autonomous except in matters affecting other groups or AA as a whole.

5. Each group has but one primary purpose—to carry the message to the alcoholic who still suffers.

6. An AA group ought never endorse, finance, or lend the AA name to any related facility or outside enterprise, lest problems of money, property, and prestige divert us from our primary purpose.

7. Every AA group should be fully self-supporting, declining outside contributions.

8. Alcoholics Anonymous should remain forever nonprofessional, but our service centers may employ special workers.

9. Alcoholics Anonymous as such ought never be organized; but we may create special board or committees solely responsible to those they serve.

10. Alcoholics Anonymous has no opinion on outside issues, hence the AA name ought never be drawn into public controversy.

11. Our public relations policy is based on attraction rather than pro-motion; we need always maintain personal anonymity at the level of press, radio, and film.

12. Anonymity is the spiritual foundation of all our traditions, ever reminding us to place principles before personalities.

An explanation of what might happen to a new member as he or she begins to "work" the program is found on page 107 of *The Twelve and Twelve*:

Step One showed us an amazing paradox: We found that we were totally unable to be rid of the alcohol obsession until we first admitted we were powerless over it.

In Step Two we saw that since we could not restore ourselves to sanity, some Higher Power must necessarily do so if we were to survive.

Consequently, in Step Three we turned our will and our lives over to the care of God as we understood Him. For the first time, we who were atheist or agnostic discovered that our own group, or AA as a whole, would suffice as a higher power. [This was the beginning of the "God Thing."]

Beginning with Step Four, we commenced to search out the things in our-selves which had brought us to physical, moral, and spiritual bankruptcy. We made a searching and moral inventory.

Looking at Step Five, we decided that an inventory, taken alone, would not be enough. We knew we would have to quit the deadly business of living alone with our conflicts, and in honesty confide these to God and another human being. [And of course, admit them to ourselves]

At Step Six, many of us balked for the practical reason that we did not wish to have all the defects of character removed, because we still loved some of them too much. Yet we knew we had to make a settlement with the fundamental principle of Step Six. So, we decided that while we still had some flaws of character that we could not yet relinquish, we ought nevertheless to quit our stubborn, rebellious hanging on to them. We said to ourselves, "This I cannot do today, perhaps, but I can stop crying out 'No, never!'"

Then in Step Seven we humbly asked God to remove our shortcomings such as He could or would under the conditions of the day we asked.

In Step Eight we continued our housecleaning, for we saw we were not only in conflict with ourselves, but also with people and situations in the world in which we lived. We had begun to make our peace, and so we listed the people we had harmed and became willing to set things right.

We followed this up in Step Nine by making direct amends to those concerned, except when to do so would injure them or other people.

By this time, at Step Ten, we had begun to get a basis of daily living, and we keenly realized that we would need to continue taking personal inventory, and that when we were wrong, we ought to admit it promptly.

In Step Eleven we saw that if a Higher Power had restored us to sanity and had enabled us to live with some peace of mind in a sorely troubled world, then such a Higher Power was worth knowing better, by as direct a contact as possible. The persistent use of meditation and prayer, we found, did open the channel so that where there had been a trickle, there was now a river which led to sure power and safe guidance from God as we were increasingly better able to understand Him.

Therefore, in Step Twelve, in practicing these steps, we had a spiritual awakening about which there was no question. *Looking at those who were only beginning and still doubted themselves, the rest of us were able to see the change setting in.* From great numbers of such experiences, we could predict that the doubter who still claimed he had not got the "spiritual angle," and who still considered his well-loved AA group the higher power would presently "love" God and call Him by name. Now, what about the rest of the Twelfth Step? The wonderful energy it releases and the eager action by which it carries our message to the next suffering alcoholic, and which finally translates the Twelve Steps into action upon all our affairs, is the payoff, the magnificent reality, of AA.

CHAPTER 39

GINNY'S PROGRAM

Ginny was having no problem with the program. She dove into it with both feet and volunteered for anything that was asked. We began to make friends and I came to enjoy AA for the social aspect the program offered. I was being accepted on an entirely different level than I had ever experienced. Strangely, I found myself becoming comfortable in AA. I had no answer or curiosity as to why.

A secret of sobriety

Ginny volunteered us to answer the telephone at AA Central. This is a service for those with a question about AA or who have an urgent and pressing need for help in their destructive drinking. With my best tool, my ability to speak well, I answered every other call and can honestly say I do not believe I was much help to anyone. Ginny, on the other hand, usually said to them, "Tell me about your drinking." She hardly had to talk at all as everyone poured out their stories to her. She could then suggest a useful resource. This methodology was not lost on me.

A secret of sobriety

CHAPTER 40

MY ALCOHOLICS ANONYMOUS PROGRAM IN THE BEGINNING

I began the program by imitating the behaviors I observed around me. I did not want to appear different. Doing what seemed necessary to have people like and admire me became my modus operandi.

A secret?

After three years in the program, with excellent help from my sponsor, I was well established with the group, especially with the men's group and Couples in Recovery. My sponsor, however, had not been able to get me to do Step 4, a searching and moral inventory. I could not seem to put my past on paper, and so began a step study, as mentioned earlier, with the help of the Thursday Night Men's Meeting.

Starting the new step study required me to attend every week, and much was expected of me. A syllabus was furnished to me: it was 121 pages long. I reacted positively to these responsibilities in order to continue to earn the respect I was beginning to receive. I had twenty copies of the syllabus made into book form. These quickly disappeared as they were so popular, and I had to break down the steps into individual copies, which we passed out at each meeting.

This was my first publishing experience.

Nevertheless, I looked good to those attending the meeting, less so to myself. Slowly I began to get the program by "assmosis," a term I devised from osmosis, where things—in this case, knowledge and experience—pass from an area of a higher concentration to that of a lower concentration through a semipermeable membrane. In this case, the aforementioned "membrane" hinted to in the term "assmosis." In other words, positive things were happening that could only be explained, in my view, empirically.

CHAPTER 41

LIFE OUTSIDE OF ALCOHOLICS ANONYMOUS

I was beginning to be involved in AA, but I was also now conducting business as a nondrinker. I was beginning to tell the truth in all my affairs. This was a major change as I had lied in the normal course of events without having a reason to. I began to be aware that people took what I was saying more seriously. I was slowly developing a reputation for being reliable. I did not become "wonderful" immediately, but the transformation had begun.

Honesty, a major secret of sobriety

Other changes were occurring in my life. I do not recall any difficulty with the dynamic of refusal when offered a drink. I went into no explanation and merely said, "No, thanks." *Ginny now had me going to church and I was introduced to the concept of grace.*

CHAPTER 42

THE INTERNATIONAL AIRCRAFT BUSINESS

TUNISIA, NORTH AFRICA

During this period, I transitioned into the international sale of large jets. These were commercial jets with more than thirty thousand landings, or cycles as they are referred to in the industry. A commercial airliner's useful life span is about sixty thousand cycles. The condition of these aircraft was much in the same order as when Hertz and Avis replace their rental cars with new ones. A Boeing 737 in this condition would sell for about $5 million, as I recall. This was about 1991. I was fifty-six.

I flew to London and met a new partner. He had somehow become aware of my reputation and had an introduction to the president of Tunisair headquartered in Tunis, Tunisia. His plan was to form a start-up company to carry freight and mail only, to be named Hercules Air. The opportunity existed as Tunisair was primarily a passenger service and carried little freight. I flew to Tunis from London to study the aviation business conditions existing in Tunisia.

SOME HISTORY OF TUNISIA

Tunisia was conquered by the French in 1881 and gained its independence in 2011. It is bordered on the southeast by Libya, on the west by Algeria, and on the north and east by the Mediterranean Sea. Its southern border is the northern Sahara Desert. Tunisia is the northernmost country in Africa.

HERCULES AIR

I had no personal in-depth knowledge of Boing 737 operations and was given the responsibility of finding an expert with the credentials to assist in the logistics and in the operating costs. I located a retired air force general who had had that responsibility while in the service. He and I flew into the Tunis-Carthage airport in Tunisia.

My partner had particularly good offices and staff, and the general and I were installed in the finest hotel in Tunis. We spent much of the first month devising a business plan involving costs, schedules, and other matters relating to starting a new airline. Yasser Arafat had his headquarters near our offices.

Tunisair was at that time, and perhaps still is, the only passenger airline that owned all its aircraft outright. They were all Boeing 727s. To learn the airline routes across Tunisair, we flew to all its destinations. Tunisia is small, less than 165,000 square miles, and had a population of less than 11 million. The capital city, Tunis, is on the North African coast with Libya to its east and Algeria to its west. This is the area of North Africa in which Rommel, the infamous German general, fought most of his well-known battles. Tunis is only about 165 miles directly across the Mediterranean Sea from Sicily. Tunis is a major port known for its Punic and Roman architectural sites. It was the seat of the powerful Carthaginian empire, which fell to Rome in the second century. Carthage is famous for its Roman ruins and for its Bible lore.

We flew from Tunis to Tozeur, which is the southernmost city in Tunisia and is in the northern part of the Sahara Desert. We spent a delightful weekend in Sousse on the west coast, a favorite vacation spot for Europeans, especially Germans. We went to a play performed in French, the second official language of Tunisia. German and English were translated. The languages in Tunisia are Tunisian Arabic, Arabic, and French.

While in Tozeur we heard a strange "plopping" sound. It was a fisherman slamming a four-foot octopus on the sidewalk in order to kill it. This occurred in a seaside area surrounded by homes of the wealthy. We visited several of these homes, and they all seemed to feature marble floors and marble walls up to about three feet.

Back in Tunis one evening, our hotel came alive with strange activity. A large line of limousines began pulling up at the hotel's side entrance. It was a delegation from Libya, and they took the entire top two floors. It seems wealthy Muslims allow themselves little breaks from their strict religion. I had noticed the same "relaxation" in Paris, a favorite vacation site for Arabs and other Middle Easterners. After a few days, they were gone, but while they were there, many attractive women also visited and orders from the bar were slower.

Of interest to me were the men's restrooms. There was, in addition to the normal facilities, a hose. Some of the men, after using the facilities, would strip and hose themselves off. They did not use their right hand. The Arabic Torah, the Tawrat, considers the right hand honorable and it cannot be used for toilet purposes, thus the hose. The men's restroom was always completely wet in our office building; probably some form of this "cleanliness" was featured all over the city.

We always went out for the evening meal, which was served late. I have often been in a restaurant at midnight when a family with young children came to eat their evening meal. There was usually a singer and the songs usually told stories about life in the desert. A camel was often prominent in the songs. Fruit was usually served at the end of the meal. My favorite dishes were the pastries, which were usually flavored with pistachio nuts or dates. Date palms were full and low enough so you could reach the fruit, not tall like in California, and of a different species.

Mediterranean meals usually featured seafood or lamb. Dinner usually featured fish, shrimp, and other seafood. Fish, shrimp, and lobster were always served with the head. Shrimp was especially enjoyed by sucking the head. I chose not to learn that technique. On balance the food was excellent.

When we finally had our sales interview with the president of Tunisair months later, it was a Saturday morning in his office. His office was not at all fancy, assuming we were invited to his primary office, and we were alone there with the president. We were well prepared with facts and figures to demonstrate Hercules Air to its best advantage, the result of months of labor. The president seemed strangely nervous. It soon became apparent he was not going to allow Hercules Air to become in any way a competitor of or companion to Tunisair. Several months of our time had been wasted at an enormous cost, but it an interesting experience. This was in the early 1990s. I was fifty-six. I in no way prospered from this transaction, nor did I suffer. This was a normal methodology of doing this type of business.

CHAPTER 43

BACK IN SAN DIEGO

After returning to San Diego from North Africa, I was again buying and selling yachts. These yachts were primarily donated to the Boy Scouts and to local universities from whom I would then purchase those donated yachts.

I was now five years "sober," or at least in recovery, and becoming more active in AA, finally gaining some respect from other AA members and even from my wife. Times were becoming good. I was becoming curious concerning AA. I had early on given AA no real thought except that I was a participant and my life was improving. Why I did not know nor was I curious.

During this period, the law changed concerning donations and the tax benefit derived due to the laxity of the law. Until this time, a yacht could be donated at its full appraised value, which was not regulated. The IRS regulations allowed a full write-off for that amount. I might buy a donated yacht from the Boy Scouts, which was donated for an appraised value of $250,000, and pay $50,000 for it. The IRS tax bracket was at that time 50 percent and the California tax added 7 percent. Therefore, the donor could claim a $142,500 write-off on his taxes that year. The law was changed to prohibit the write-off from exceeding the actual sales price, which was of course proper.

CHAPTER 44

With the new IRS law, my business was no longer viable, Ginny insisted I undergo psychological testing to determine which profession I should join. I did so and was found to be superior in several surprising professions other than sales: law, teaching, and serving as a pastor. I tested as off the chart on abstract thinking. I did not know what that meant.

My options were not practical, it seemed, as I would need extensive and expensive training. I chose instead to pursue a degree in alcohol and drug counseling, in which I had now become interested. I graduated at age sixty-two with honors and am still paying back student loans.

CHAPTER 45

COMMENTS ON INTELLIGENCE

I also, as a matter of curiosity (and ego, no doubt), took the Mensa test. It was carefully administered in San Diego. The other persons taking the tests were quite diverse. One was a man in a tuxedo wearing tennis shoes and no shirt. Others were less odd, but not what I was expecting. I believe many were taking the test for reasons of ego; soon the results came in the mail. I had passed. Mensa scores are based on two areas: one favors language and science, and the other logic. My scores were 141 and 151. I do not recall on which one I did best, nor did I understand they were high scores.

I was invited to Mensa party, and what a wacky bunch the other attendees were. One license plate read "My IQ 180." That was the only Mensa party I attended. They were not my type. I learned later the average IQ of the general public is 100 and that 68 percent of the population falls between 85 and 115. The average college graduate has an IQ of 120. I learned it requires an IQ of 130 to qualify for Mensa, which is in the upper 2 percent. Albert Einstein had an IQ of 160. The highest recorded IQ is 212, a woman. The youngest Mensa member at the time was 4 years old, the oldest 101. The IQs of our recent presidents range from 131 to 147. Earlier presidents' scores are not available.

CHAPTER 46

MENTAL CHALLENGES AND EDUCATION

During this period of testing, it was discovered I had ADHD and mild obsessive compulsive disorder (OCD). These issues had influenced my learning ability and I had to learn to compensate for these disorders. Doctors prescribed medications such as Ritalin and Wellbutrin. I soon stopped taking drugs for ADHD as I learned exercise and relearning reading skills were my best solutions. I took no drugs for OCD, and my recovery seemed to abate the disorder, although Ginny and I laugh at each other as I will arrange things neatly and she prefers things more "artistic."

I had a lot of natural curiosity concerning my mental ability and mental ability in general. I was aware of many who seemed smarter than I believed myself to be. I was to learn that IQ demonstrates itself in many ways. Many with lower IQs than mine had much higher accomplishments. My extremely poor educational background and impulsivity made me unaware I was in any way gifted, except perhaps with arrogance, impulsivity, and aggressiveness. IQ was no indicator of my or anyone else's value to the community. Many of average ability and IQ are better adjusted to life's circumstances than those who are more gifted. Some with enormous IQs can hardly dress themselves, often due to no interest in normal activities. Nevertheless, after returning to college I earned a GPA of 3.8 and graduated at age sixty-two, as earlier noted. I attribute my progress to sobriety and learning to compensate for ADHD—an amazing change from my earlier years in college has been the result.

CHAPTER 47

WHERE DID THIS BOOK COME FROM?

Whatever my reasoning, I developed a desire to understand AA and why and how it works. I also determined to better understand what in AA I refer to as the "God Thing." The "God Thing" will be discussed in more detail toward the end of this treatise.

Could the "God Thing" be something like what in Christianity is known as grace?

Early in my sobriety, during an AA meeting I attended regularly, I met a gentleman who was intrigued with some of my sharing. His name was Alfred Heck. Al was the author of three books, all about the people in Germany, especially the youth, during World War II. Al was a member of the Nazi Youth Corps who toward the end of the war was sent to glider school. Al received a medal from Hitler personally. When the war ended, he did not believe the stories about Hitler and the German regime and went to Nuremberg to attend the war trials. There he discovered the truth of Nazi Germany's behavior. He was so distressed he left Germany and immigrated to Canada and eventually to San Diego.

Al was constantly on me about writing a book. "Bob," he said, "a page a day and in a year, you will have a book." I therefore dedicate this writing to Alfred Heck, now in the "meeting in the sky." I must ask, Al, was not your advice an oversimplification? I did not begin this book for publication. And perhaps it will not be published. I began my research in order to codify my own understanding of AA. I began to read and reread everything I had read about AA. I soon learned the depth of my ignorance and began real research. What follows is some of what I have learned. I have tried to make it readable, as every reader will not have as deep an interest in AA as I found I had. Some suggested I add personal information, and I have.

CHAPTER 48

HISTORY OF ALCOHOLISM

Philippus Aureolus Bombastus von Hohenheim coined the word *alcohol* in 1530. It came from the Arabic *alkuhl*, which means delicate flower. The earlier expression was *spiritus vini*.

The terms *alcoholic* and *alcoholism* were first used in 1848 by Swedish scientist Magnus Hess. Earlier, the condition was referred to as chronic or continual drunkenness. The sufferer was known as a drunkard or an inebriate.

The use and/or misuse of the word *alcohol* is as old as recorded history. It is referred to biblically in the Old and New Testaments. The Bible suggests alcohol, primarily wine, was approved socially, although wine was both alcoholic and nonalcoholic. Abuse of alcohol was not approved, and abstinence was the suggested solution if abuse became a problem.

Alcohol abuse has also been a concern from the earliest records. Treatment of the abuser was often severe. The Turks allowed pouring molten lead down the throat of an abuser of alcohol, or an alcoholic; imprisonment was normal *as abuse was considered a choice*. The abuser was sometimes considered insane and committed to an insane asylum or prison. The varieties of treatment and punishment for the alcoholic are too numerous to list here as a complete history would require a book by itself and would not be useful for this purpose.

In 1785, Dr. Benjamin Rush, in his "Inquiry into the Effects of Ardent Spirits," postulated drunkards were addicted to "spiritus liquor" and became addicted gradually and progressively. He declared the condition a disease. It was not considered a disease in the United States until the American Medical Association, the AMA, declared it as such in 1956. At about the same period, an English doctor named Thomas Trotter concurred in his "Essay: Medical, Philosophical, and Chemical." He wrote, "In medical language, I consider drunkenness, strictly speaking, as a disease caused by a remote cause." The meaning of Dr. Trotter's "caused by a remote cause" is to this day a puzzling question. These are the first records I found in my research of the perception of alcoholism as a disease.

In any event, historically, medically, psychologically, philosophically, and religiously, alcoholics, as they came to be named, were quietly ignored as beyond any known help. The doctor and the psychiatrist had tried everything within their training with no positive result and had finally to resort to institutionalizing or treating each incident with no real belief the outcome would affect a "cure." The religious man tried prayer and counseling to no serious effect; the alcoholic continued drinking. A great psychiatrist of the day, Dr. Carl Jung, believed only a spiritual solution could stop an alcoholic from destructive drinking.

A spiritual solution? Keep this thought in mind. A secret of sobriety.

CHAPTER 49

THE EIGHTEENTH AMENDMENT: PROHIBITION

The problem became acute enough here in the United States that the Eighteenth Amendment, Prohibition, became the law of the land in 1920, making alcohol illegal. The noble experiment failed, and the Eighteenth Amendment was repealed in 1933. Prohibition made millionaires of gangsters and taught the average man to make bathtub gin. Although the fundamental intention of prohibition had been to curb drunkenness by outlawing liquor, the opposite was realized. Drinking achieved a certain cachet. It became an "in thing" to drink and outsmart the authorities.

CHAPTER 50

THE WASHINGTONIANS AND THE OXFORD GROUP

Drinking once again became accepted after prohibition was repealed, but drunkards were still not. Chronic alcoholism was still considered a moral weakness or a sin. The idea that alcoholism was an illness, and that complete abstinence was necessary, was not considered a solution, although the theory was proffered in the early 1800s by Surgeon General Benjamin Rush and by others, as previously noted. All things considered, conquering the compelling nature of alcoholism is and has been daunting to the point of impossibility for all professions, organizations, religions, and individuals over the ages. The conception of AA was considered the most significant spiritual event of the past century. It was perhaps the Gallup Poll that revealed that the establishment of AA was the eighty-eighth most important happening of any kind in the past century.

THE WASHINGTONIANS

A near exception was the Washingtonians, a total abstinence society founded in 1840 by six alcoholics in Maryland. The original idea was that by relying on each other, sharing their alcoholic experience, and creating an atmosphere of conviviality, they could keep each other sober. Total abstinence from alcohol (teetotalism) was their goal. The group taught sobriety and preceded AA by nearly a century.

Members sought out other "drunkards" (the term *alcoholic* had not yet been coined) and told them their own experience with alcohol and how the society had helped them achieve sobriety. The society became a prohibitionist organization in that it promoted the legal and mandatory prohibition of alcoholic beverages.

I was not able to find how they chose the name. Their idea that relying on each other, sharing their alcoholic experiences, and creating an atmosphere of conviviality could keep each other sober had much merit, and the society grew to as many as six hundred thousand members. Many of these concepts were later found in the AA program, not, however, from historic knowledge of the group or its principles.

The Washingtonians used big names, of which there were many, to further their cause. Abraham Lincoln reportedly spoke at an event. Unfortunately, many of these notables slipped back into drinking, damaging the image of the group. The Washingtonians also became fragmented in their primary purpose of sobriety, becoming involved in social reform, prohibition, sectarian religion, and abolition of slavery. These practices led to the deterioration of the singleness of purpose once so clearly evident. The society became so thoroughly forgotten that fifty years later, neither cofounder of AA had even heard of the Washingtonians, although comparisons are often made of the two groups due to their similarities.

Singleness of purpose, a secret of sobriety

THE OXFORD GROUP

Another group had a more important effect on AA; that group came to be known as the Oxford Group and was formed by Frank Buchman. Frank Buchman was an aggressive and ambitious young man who became a Lutheran minister at age twenty-four. He dreamed of being assigned to a large, important church but was instead given a non-prestigious posting in a Philadelphia suburb.

Within three years, Buchanan built the church into a vigorous success but differences emerged between Buchanan and the governing board. He resigned in resentment over his "unjust" treatment and, financed by his parents, went abroad, where he attended the 1908 Keswick Convention, an annual gathering of evangelical Christians in Cumbria, England. There, he was moved by the preaching of Jessie Penn-Lewis.

Her message moved him to write letters of apology to the board with whom he had issues that led to his resignation. In the letter of apology, he took ownership of his prideful behavior in holding resentments. Relief from these "amends" brought him a spiritual experience that would later influence the principles of the yet unnamed Oxford Group,

Amends, another secret of sobriety

In 1928, Frank Buchman's "association" became known as the Oxford Group, no doubt for the prestige of the name. Due to his history of conflict with institutional authority, he vowed the Oxford Group would be a voice of protest against organized and lifeless Christian work of doctrinal and institution-based religion. Among the principles of this new Oxford Group *was absolute surrender, guidance by the Holy Spirit, sharing bringing about true fellowship, and life-changing faith and prayer.* The Oxford Group aimed for absolute standards of love, purity, honesty, and unselfishness, all of which came into being in the AA program.

Secrets of sobriety in principle

The group gained a solid following that included Reverend Sam Shoemaker. He became Buchman's right-hand man and the leader of the American group. Reverend Shoemaker became the episcopal rector at Calvary Church in New York City, which came to operate the Calvary Rescue Mission. The Calvary Rescue Mission and Buchanan's relationship with Reverend Shoemaker were to become important in AA's early years. This group influenced Bill Wilson's early work.

CHAPTER 51

THE EARLY DAYS OF (PRE-)ALCOHOLICS ANONYMOUS IN AKRON, OHIO, AND NEW YORK CITY

Akron, Ohio, was the great center for tire manufacturing in North America and where the cofounders of AA, Bill Wilson and Dr. Robert Smith, met. The Oxford Group of Akron assisted Russell "Bud" Firestone in conquering a severe drinking problem. His father, Harvey, the founder of Firestone Tires, had four things the Oxford Group liked: *wealth, fame, generosity, and gratitude*.

The rubber magnate, in his appreciation for his son's sobriety, hosted a ten-day gala in January 1933 that brought the Oxford Group to the forefront of Akron society. This set the stage for the famous Mother's Day meeting between Bill W. and Dr. Bob on May 12, 1935.

CARL JUNG

In New York, during that same period, a wealthy mill owner and state senator had a son with a severe alcohol problem. He was Rowland H. Hazard III, and he sought the help of world-famous psychiatrist Carl Jung in Switzerland. Dr. Jung, after two unsuccessful treatments, told Rowland Hazard to go home and possibly find sobriety through some religious group. Dr. Jung had come to believe only a spiritual event could bring about sobriety. Rowland Hazard did as advised; he found the Oxford Group in New York, which was successful in achieving his recovery. *There it is again, a spiritual event.*

CHAPTER 52

EBBY THATCHER AND SAM SHOEMAKER

Ebby Thatcher, also during this time period, a childhood friend of Bill W.'s, was about to be locked up as a chronic drunk in Bennington, Vermont. He was visited by three men from the Oxford Group that included Rowland Hazard. They, due to their wealth and influence, persuaded the judge to parole Ebby, a wealthy contemporary, to their care. They sent Ebby to the Calvary Mission in New York City, where Sam Shoemaker was rector, and the Oxford Group had its American home. *This is a subtle example of the "God Thing." Consider the concept.*

Ebby was taught, in summary, that

> *You admit you are licked.*

> *You get honest with yourself.*

> *You talk it out with somebody else.*

You make restitution to the people you have harmed.

> *You try to give of yourself without stint, with no demand for reward, and you pray to whatever god you think there is, even as an experiment.*

These are some of the basic principles of the Oxford Group which were to influence the twelve steps of AA.

BILL WILSON

Born on November 26, 1895, in Dorset, Vermont, William Griffith Wilson was abandoned by his parents when he was a child. His father never returned, and his mother left to study osteopathic medicine. Bill and his sister were raised by their maternal grandparents. His paternal grandfather was an alcoholic who never drank again after a "conversion" experience, although history draws no conclusions.

As a teen, Bill was a determined young man, and after some difficulties, he became the captain of the school's football team as well as the principal violinist of the school orchestra. Bill's childhood sweetheart, whom he had planned to marry, died suddenly, and Bill fell into serious depression. This depression was to follow him throughout his life.

Later, in 1913, Bill met his wife to be, Lois Burnham, and they became engaged two years later. Bill became a student at Norwich University, but depression and panic attacks caused his withdrawal.

BILL'S MILITARY

The 1916 incursion of Poncho Villa across the American border brought General John Pershing into the conflict and causing Bill Wilson's class to be mobilized. As a result, he was reinstated to serve with his class. World War I began, and so did Bill Wilson's military career. During his military training, Bill had his first drink, a glass of beer, to little effect. Soon afterward he had a Bronx cocktail and immediately felt at ease in society for the first time. "I have found the 'elixir of life,'" he said. That first time, he got thoroughly drunk and passed out completely.

LOIS WILSON

Bill married Lois in 1918 and served as a second lieutenant in the Coast Artillery. He served in Europe and believed his service experience would serve him well in his career after the war. It was not to be. After his military service, his drinking brought about his failure to graduate from law school. He was too drunk to pick up his diploma.

CHAPTER 53

EARLY CAREER

Bill became a stock speculator and did well evaluating companies for potential investors. He traveled the country on a motorcycle with Lois sometimes in the sidecar and sometimes driving. His reviews of the companies he investigated gained him a favorable reputation. His drinking, however, made success impossible and began ruining his long-term hope for success. His drinking continued for years and grew worse and worse— he simply could not control or stop his drinking.

Bill next attempted to build a career on Wall Street. He worked on Wall Street until the Great Depression in 1929 put him out of work. The as yet unnamed disease of alcoholism exerted an even stronger pull. He was given a reprieve from a friend in Canada who put him to work. Nevertheless, he was quickly back to his old lifestyle, which soon caused his drinking to escalate to the point where he was fired. Bill and Lois were forced to return to New York and move in with Lois's parents. Bill was to have no real employment for five years, and hardly drew a sober breath. Lois took a job at a department store only to return each evening from work to find Bill drunk. Bill became an unwelcome hanger-on at local brokerages.

ALCOHOL THE WINNER

Liquor was no longer a luxury—it had become a necessity. Bill, because of the price, had to drink "bathtub" gin, at least two and sometimes three bottles a day. Soon Bill would awaken each day shaking violently and would have to swallow a large tumbler of gin and many beers.

This episode lasted another two years. His condition grew more serious, and he dared not even go out on the street.

Bill finally again renewed his resolve to "control his drinking," and some time passed. He became confident he had finally beat drinking alcohol. He became cocky. *I can laugh at gin mills. Now*, he thought, *I have what it takes.*

Sometime later, after working steadily for a time, Bill walked into a bar to make a call and have a bite to eat. Without a thought he ordered a whisky with his lunch. Soon he had had several and began to wonder what had happened. *Oh well, I might as well get drunk as long as I have had one.*

When he sobered up this time, however, Bill began to finally realize and admit he had a problem. "I cannot even have one drink. I am through forever. This time I mean business," Bill said, and so he did. Occasional periods of sobriety made Bill believe he could control his drinking and gave Lois hope. It was not to last. Bill and Lois Wilson were about to learn the truth about alcoholism.

CHAPTER 54

HELP ARRIVES, EBBY MEETS BILL

The next chapter in the history of AA came when Ebby Thatcher, fresh from his own experience with the Oxford Group, asked Bill if he could visit. Bill agreed and Ebby arrived at his apartment, where Bill was drinking gin. Lois was at work in the department store. Bill welcomed Ebby as an old friend and offered him a drink. Ebby refused and told Bill he had "got religion" and shared with Bill his story. Bill was not impressed on the spot, but it was part of his memory when his drinking took him to the Charles Townes Hospital.

THE CHARLES TOWNES HOSPITAL

Bill's sister Dorothy's husband was a physician in New York, and because of empathy and concern for his wife's brother, placed Bill in the Charles Townes Hospital. There he began to learn something of the disease of alcoholism through the efforts of a kind doctor, William Silkworth.

DR. WILLIAM SILKWORTH, A PATRON OF AA

Sobriety lasted several months, and then Bill drank again—this time he nearly died. Another hospital visit. Another period of sobriety. On Armistice Day in 1934, Bill drank again. Bill was soon readmitted to the hospital. While there, he overheard the doctor tell Lois he would soon die or be admitted permanently to a center for incurable alcoholics. This was in December 1934.

Facing this, Bill finally asked God for help. Those details will be revealed later.

CHAPTER 55

CHARLES TOWNES HOSPITAL AND DR. SILKWORTH

The Charles Townes Hospital, located on 293 Central Park West, NYC, was founded in 1901, and was famous as a rich man's rehabilitation clinic serving a worldwide clientele: American millionaires, European royalty, and oil sheiks walked its halls in humiliation and bedroom slippers. Dr. William Duncan Silkworth, famous for his treatment of alcoholics, was the director. The fees were well beyond Bill and Lois Wilsons's ability, but *the visits were "sponsored" by Dr. Leonard Strong. Dr. Strong was married to Bill's sister Dorothy and later was to become important as a stalwart of AA.* Eventually, after even more severe bouts with alcohol, Bill was back in Townes for treatment. As reported, during his fourth visit, which was to be his last, *he was showing signs of delirium tremens.*

CHAPTER 56

A BIT ABOUT ALCOHOL

An explanation of the eventual result of chronic alcoholism might be appropriate at this time. Heavy daily drinking disrupts the brain's production of neurotransmitters, chemicals in the brain that transmit messages throughout the body.

Alcohol initially enhances the effects of GABA, the neurotransmitter that produces the feeling of relaxation and calm, hence one of the appeals of drinking alcohol. Chronic alcohol consumption, however, eventually suppresses GABA activity so that more and more alcohol is necessary to achieve the same effect; this phenomenon came to be known as "tolerance."

Chronic alcohol consumption also suppresses the activity of glutamate, the neurotransmitter that produces the feeling of excitability. To maintain equilibrium, when alcohol is taken in excess, the glutamate system responds by functioning at a far higher level than for moderate or non-drinkers. Therefore, when a heavy drinker stops drinking, the neurotransmitters previously suppressed are no longer suppressed, resulting in brain hyperactivity, anxiety, irritability, agitation, tremors, and delirium tremors (DTs). *These are obvious fact of alcoholism.*

CHAPTER 57

A HOPELESS ALCOHOLIC

It was during this fourth visit that Bill overheard Dr. Silkworth tell Lois he was a hopeless alcoholic and he would either die or be institutionalized for a wet brain. Wet brain is a condition brought about by a deficiency of thiamine. Its technical name is Wernicke-Korsakoff syndrome, a common medical name for a parallel effect of some with severe alcoholism.

Earlier that day, Ebby had visited Bill and tried to convince Bill to turn himself over to the care of the Oxford Group, who, Ebby claimed, would liberate him from alcohol. The fact that Ebby had remained sober had made an impression on Bill, as Ebby, in Bill's opinion, had a more severe drinking problem than his own. The conversation that stayed in his memory was Ebby saying, "Bill, it isn't a bit like being on the water wagon. You do not fight the desire to drink, you get released from it. I never had such a feeling before." (The phrase "water wagon" came from the old American West where cowboys spent much of their pay on liquor in town at the saloons. Upon returning to the range, these cowpokes spent much of the first day on the "water wagon"—i.e., next to the chuck wagon, hydrating.)

More important, Ebby's statements, combined with Dr. Silkworth's earlier statements to Lois, so depressed Bill that it finally seemed as though he was at the bottom of the pit: in the AA lexicon, Bill had hit his bottom. *Hitting bottom, another secret of sobriety.*

CHAPTER 58

BILL WILSON'S "WHITE LIGHT" EXPERIENCE

Ebby's suggestions no longer seemed unreasonable. Although Bill still gagged at the idea of a power greater than himself, just for the moment the last vestige of his proud obstinacy was crushed and, in Bill's words: *"All at once I found myself crying out, if there is a god, let Him show Himself. I am ready to do anything, anything; suddenly the room lit up with a great white light. I was caught up in an ecstasy, of which there are no words to describe. It seemed to me, in my mind's eye, that I was on a mountain and that a wind, not of air, but of spirit was blowing. And then it burst on me that I was a free man. Now for a time I was in another world, a new world of consciousness. All about me was a wonderful feeling of Presence, and I thought to myself, 'So this is the god of the preachers.' A great peace stole over me."* This occurred in December 1934, which became Bill W's sobriety date. This was not to be an experience I was to have—a "white light" experience— and it is difficult for me to comprehend. Nevertheless, it also happened to Ginny, and it happened to others, although rarely.

LOSING THE PINK CLOUD

Then, little by little, Bill began to be frightened. His education told him he was hallucinating and that this was merely a psychological phenomenon. This was an experience I was to have and that often happened to others. It is common for the beginning of relapse.

A fact of early sobriety

This phenomenon is common in early sobriety—in the period after "the pink cloud" passes, the alcoholic begins to rethink his new sobriety and search for another solution.

BILL BELIEVES THE DOCTOR

Luckily, Bill transcended this thought and told himself he had better get the doctor. He did so, and Dr. Silkworth asked him a lot of questions. After a while, he said, "No, Bill, you are not crazy. There has been some basic psychological or spiritual event here. I have read about these things in some medical books."

Sometimes spiritual experiences do release people from alcoholism. Dr. Carl Jung, the world-famous psychiatrist, was one of Dr. Silkworth's sources. Dr. William James, who Bill later credited as one of the founders of AA, was another.

An example of a spiritual experience toward recovery—food for thought!

While Bill was still in the hospital, someone brought him Dr. James's book *Varieties of Religious Experiences*, through which he learned spiritual experiences can make people saner and transform men and women so that they can do, feel, and believe what had hitherto been impossible to them. Dr. James said it matters little whether these spiritual awakenings are sudden like Bill W.'s or gradual. Their variety could be almost infinite, hence the title: "Varieties of Religious Experiences." *Mine was to be of the educational variety.*

Some, without believing "the fact of religious experiences," come to believe that those presenting these beliefs did believe, and therefore have accepted their belief. In most of these cases, those who had been transformed were hopeless alcoholics. Bill W. credits Dr. Silkworth, Dr. William James, the Oxford Group, and Reverend Sam Shoemaker for having the most influence in the development of AA. The fleshing out of the program occurred as AA developed slowly, a day at a time over several years.

CHAPTER 59

BILL'S EARLY RECOVERY AND THE BIRTH OF ALCOHOLICS ANONYMOUS

Bill then became involved in the Oxford Group, with its director, Sam Shoemaker, at the Calvary Mission, and began working with drunks most every day. Bill focused on service to the alcoholics. Sam Shoemaker worked closely with Bill and reinforced the principles of the Oxford Group. Nevertheless, Bill had not succeeded in getting one man sober. *This result, I believe, was due to using only the principles of the Oxford Group, which were evangelical only, without the new principles yet to be developed, those of scientific fact. Stay tuned!*

As Bill's health improved, he began to re-involve himself in the financial market. He had some small successes in the market, but no success in his efforts in the field of recovery.

His efforts in the financial market, however, earned Bill a business opportunity in Akron, Ohio. After a time, the venture lost momentum and Bill found himself away from his home and his safe environment at Calvary Mission in NYC.

THE ADVENT OF ALCOHOLICS ANONYMOUS

On Mother's Day in May 1935, Bill found himself alone in the lobby of the Mayflower Hotel in Akron. The sounds from the bar began to appeal to his old nature. He was sorely tempted to have "a ginger ale" and scrape up an acquaintance. "Then I panicked," Bill said. "I remembered that in my trying to help others, I had stayed sober myself, and for the first time I deeply realized it. I thought, 'You need another alcoholic to talk to; you need another alcoholic just as much as he needs you.'" *This is another secret of AA.*

Choosing at random from the church directory in the lobby, Bill eventually reached a pastor, Walter Tanks, later a friend of AA, who gave him the name of Henrietta Seiberling of the Seiberling Tire Company family and a member of the Akron Oxford Group. Ms. Seiberling told Bill of Dr. Bob Smith and arranged for a meeting of the two *who were to become the cofounders of AA, Bill Wilson, and Dr. Bob Smith.* Dr. Bob's wife, Anne, who was involved in the Oxford Group and had been working for years to get her husband sober, was a close friend of Henrietta Seiberling.

CHAPTER 60

MEET DR. ROBERT HOLBROOK SMITH

Dr. Bob, Robert Holbrook Smith, was a physician and surgeon born in Vermont. His was a religious family who were at church every time the door was open. This may have been the onset of his "drug" and alcohol problem, as he was "drug" to church every time the door was open. As a young man, Bob resolved to never again attend a religious service.

Bob attended Dartmouth College, where his drinking began. His drinking very nearly caused him to fail his college work. Nevertheless, after graduation, and several years selling hardware, he returned to college to study medicine, but his drinking began to cause him to miss classes. He left school but returned and passed his exams for his sophomore year. He then transferred to Rush Medical College and his drinking caused him to have a dismal showing during final exams, but the college agreed to graduate him if he attended an additional two quarters and would remain sober during that time. He did so. After graduation, his internship left little time for drinking.

He married Anne Ripley and opened a practice in colorectal surgery. He soon returned to heavy drinking and, whether on his own or due to Anne's concern, over the years turned himself into more than a dozen hospitals and sanatoriums in an attempt to stop his alcoholic drinking.

Prohibition helped, but he soon learned that medicinal alcohol and bootleggers more than enabled him to drink excessively. For seventeen years, he battled his inability and Anne's effort to stop his drinking, and to hold together a medical practice in which his drinking became well known in the community and sorely affected his practice and his earning ability.

CHAPTER 61

DR. BOB AND BILL W MEET

Before Dr. Bob and Bill W. met, Bill began to realize he had had no success in helping anyone to stop drinking. He recalled that just before leaving for Akron, Dr. Silkworth had given him a great bit of advice. Without it, AA might never have been born.

"Look, Bill," he had said. *"You are having nothing but failure because you are preaching at these alcoholics. You are talking to them about the Oxford Group precepts, of being honest, pure, unselfish, and absolutely loving. This is a big order. Then you top it off by harping on this mysterious spiritual experience of yours. No wonder they point their finger to their heads and go out and get drunk. Aren't you the same fellow who showed me that deflation at great depth is the foundation of most spiritual experiences? No Bill, you have the horse before the cart. You have got to deflate these people first and then give them the medical business hard. Pour it into them about the obsession that condemns them to drink and the physical sensitivity or allergy of the body that condemns them to go mad or die if they continue drinking. These facts, coming from another alcoholic, one alcoholic talking to another, maybe that will crack those tough egos down deep. Only then can you begin to try out your other medicine, God, and the ethical principles you have picked up from the Oxford Group."*

This is another secret of sobriety and the importance of Dr. Silkworth to the AA program.

"The next day, talking with Dr. Bob, I remembered all that Dr. Silkworth had said. So I went very slowly on the fireworks about God and my religious experience. I just talked about my own case until he got a good identification with me, until he was moved to say, 'Yes that'd be me, I'm like that.'" Then Dr. Bob told Bill his story, a breakthrough for Dr. Bob. *An important secret of sobriety.*

CHAPTER 62

ALCOHOLICS ANONYMOUS BEGINS: JUNE 10, 1935

They met nearly every day for weeks and Dr. Bob did not drink.

In the first week of June, Dr. Bob needed to go to a medical meeting in Atlanta. He did not return on schedule and finally after several days his nurse called with the news Dr. Bob was at her house drunk. Anne and Bill picked him up and began sobering him up. He had a surgery scheduled June 10 and would need days to recover. On the day of his surgery, Bill gave Dr. Bob a beer to calm his nerves, and Dr. Bob left to perform the operation. Hours later, he called; all had gone well. But rather than returning immediately, he had gotten into his car and visited his creditors and others he had harmed by his behavior. That was June 10, 1935. To the time of his death fifteen years later, Dr. Bob never had another drink of alcohol. *His first amends. Amends: regret for past behavior. Another secret of sobriety. And now Step 9*

CHAPTER 63

ALCOHOLICS ANONYMOUS IS BORN

This became the birth of AA, although it was not so named until 1939. Until then it was a group of rebels attending the Oxford Group meetings with an entirely different agenda than that of the Oxford Group—the desire to stop drinking.

Interestingly, today we celebrate an AA birthday on the first day we did not drink. Dr. Bob had a beer on the first day AA is celebrated, although it was to steady his nerves for the operation.

The next day, Dr. Bob said, "Bill, don't you think working on other alcoholics is terribly important? We would be much safer if we got active, wouldn't we?" Bill said yes, but asked, "Where would we find any alcoholics?"

Dr. Bob called a nurse friend at Akron City Hospital, Sister Ignatia whom you will soon meet, and explained a friend from New York had a "cure for alcoholism." She knew Dr. Bob of old and asked, "Have you tried it on yourself?"

"Yes," he said. "I sure have." Sister Ignatia, as time went on, played an important part in the development of AA.

CHAPTER 64

THE AGE OF ALCOHOLICS ANONYMOUS

Thus began the age of AA, although it was yet to be so named. Bill Wilson and Dr. Bob Smith spent the next several months working on the new AA program, which in its infancy was primarily one alcoholic talking to another alcoholic.

Their first customer was in no shape to be seen that day, but they were able to see him the next day. He was interested in the information about the allergy and the obsession, but balked on the spiritual grounds. "I believe in God," he said. "I was a deacon in my church. I am too far gone for that. I have been in this place six times in the last four months. I am afraid to go home; I would get drunk." *An introduction to the "God Thing." A secret of sobriety.*

They asked if they could come again, and he agreed. When they returned, he told his wife, Henrietta: "These are the fellows I was telling you about. They are the ones who know. They understand what this thing is about." He then told them that during the night, hope had dawned on him. If Bob could do it, so could he. Maybe we can do together what we could not do separately. *Another secret of sobriety.*

Two days later, he walked out of the hospital and never drank again. He was AA number three. Ernie was number four. By summer's end, there were two more. Dr. Bob and Bill W., ably assisted by his wife, Anne, and Henrietta Seiberling, continued working with alcoholics through the venue of the Oxford Group.

I do not pretend the details presented comprise all the details of the early days of AA, but I am comfortable that what I have written is credible.

CHAPTER 65

SISTER IGNATIA

The history of AA would not be complete without the acknowledgment of the contribution of Sister Ignatia. Sister Ignatia, born Della Mary Gavin, first served as a novitiate in St. Vincent's Orphanage in Cleveland, Ohio.

She had had musical training and became a much-respected music teacher. After seven happy years, a change in administration greatly affected her and she became depressed and ill. She managed to overcome her ills and due to her musical experience was sent to the University of Notre Dame, where she received a bachelor of arts degree in music. This was 1925. She was thirty-six.

Sister Ignatia was thrown into an impossible schedule for several years. She was frail, overworked, and underappreciated by certain superiors and fell ill again suffering paralysis and a psychological breakdown.

Enter Dr. Frank Duran, a physician, diagnostician, internist, and well-versed practitioner in psychiatric medicine. Dr. Duran was an early member of the Society of Medical Psychiatry and the American Society of Hypnosis. After a long treatment featuring all of Dr. Duran's skill's, he reviewed the balance of Sister Ignatia's extremely heavy work schedule, much of it self-motivated, and her love of music, and told her, "Sister Ignatia, you can either be a live nun or a dead musician."

Then a miracle happened. Total surrender to Dr. Duran's advice freed Sister Ignatia and transformed her life. For the next decade or so she extended herself to others, guaranteeing her own recovery and faith. *Service, a secret inside and outside of AA.*

It was in 1935 that Dr. Bob, Sister Ignatia, and Bill W. met. Dr. Bob knew of Sister Ignatia from the Akron City Hospital and had studied her exemplary traits; a friendship grew into an enduring relationship of service to others. While Bill W. returned to New York to continue his work there, Dr.

Bob and Sister Ignatia achieved five thousand recoveries from alcoholism by the time of Dr. Bob's death in 1950.

Much of Sister Ignatia's success was a result of being the admissions nurse. As such she was able to bend normal rules and essentially admit an alcoholic who would not meet normal admission requirements. She put some admissions in closets until other facilities became available. Her methods were extraordinary and caused her problems with the staff continually. If not for her amazing success, she would have been disciplined.

Sister Ignatia was transferred to Cleveland, where at several hospitals, including St. Vincent Charity Hospital, it has been reported she achieved thousands more recoveries. She, with Dr. Bob, had an amazing 93 percent recovery rate. Bill W. called her involvement a divine conspiracy and she was named the "Angel of AA." These are incredible accomplishments, but she was without doubt extraordinary.

CHAPTER 66

EARLY ALCOHOLICS ANONYMOUS ISSUES

Both cofounders, due to their drinking, had severe financial problems. Bill's money had run out by this time while he was in Akron, and he returned to New York. Endowed with more humility, more understanding, and more experience, Bill slowly began developing a group in New York. Bill and Lois took alcoholics into their home, housing and feeding as many as five at a time. They expected to pick up a lot of knowledge: knowledge they gained, along with death, disorder, and suicides among those they were trying to help. Bill and Lois soon learned if they permitted alcoholics to become too dependent on them, they were apt to stay drunk. This was the beginning of the concept of codependency, *a secret of sobriety, perhaps*.

CHAPTER 67

EARLY SUCCESS

Work continued despite failures, some in Sam Shoemaker's Oxford Group, some at Calvary Chapel, and some at the Charles Townes Hospital, where Dr. Silkworth risked his reputation by letting Bill see his patients. That fall of 1935, a weekly meeting in Bill and Lois's parlor in Brooklyn started, and despite much early failure, a solid group finally developed.

Two early successes were Henry P. and Fritz M. from the Charles Townes Hospital. Both had a special impact as time went on. More recoveries followed. Akron and now Cleveland were having even more success, especially Cleveland, where certain events were occurring that will be discussed later. Cleveland is only a few miles from Akron, and some from Cleveland were members of the early Akron group.

CHAPTER 68

SEPARATION FROM THE OXFORD GROUP IN NEW YORK

The New York group had worked alongside the Oxford Group, but parted company with these great friends in mid-1937. The Oxford Group's objective was Christian salvation, and its members did not think highly of the special objective of working only with alcoholics. Additionally, the Oxford Group did not allow Catholics as members, and the Catholic Church did not allow members to have an association with another religious organization; as many Catholics were in need of sobriety, this was an important issue.

CHAPTER 69

THE ALCOHOLICS ANONYMOUS PROGRAM DEVELOPS

The Oxford Group had clearly shown Bill W. and Dr. Bob which of their principles worked in the recovery of alcoholics. As important, AA was shown what not to do as far as alcoholics are concerned, especially from the Christian religious view. Many of their ideas and attitudes simply could not be sold to alcoholics, especially in early recovery. Alcoholics, pre-recovery, seemed unable to take pressure and stress in any form. It had become apparent that the two groups had serious differences. Alcoholics only wanted to become sober; they clung to their defects and were only able to let them go one by one and slowly at that. The AA method of "progress, not perfection" was just being developed. The Oxford Group concepts of absolute purity, absolute honesty, absolute unselfishness, and absolute love were usually too much for the drunks in early recovery. The Oxford Group preferred public prominence while AA was beginning to recognize that *anonymity* was essential to its success; it was important to those in early recovery that their recovery was their private business.

Progress not perfection and anonymity are secrets of sobriety. Anonymity allo The Oxford Group preferred public prominence while AA was beginning to recognize that anonymity was essential to its success; it was important to those in early recovery that their recovery was their private business. wed the alcoholic to be private in recovery. Privacy was an important issue in the amelioration of shame, usually an issue with the recovering man or woman, although there was only one woman among the first one hundred AA members.

CHAPTER 70

AKRON LEAVES THE OXFORD GROUP

In Akron, the "alcoholic group" was more closely defined by the Oxford Group and did not separate until 1939. Sam Shoemaker, the American leader of the Oxford Group, left the organization in 1941, but remained an important and lasting friend of AA.

Akron gained membership faster than New York. perhaps due to the activity of Sister Ignatia and Dr. Bob's large group of "prospects." Nevertheless, Cleveland exceeded both groups, a story to be developed later.

CHAPTER 71

SIGNS OF GROWTH

An opportunity came in Cleveland for Bill, and while he was there, this adjacency to Akron brought him back into much closer contact with Dr. Bob. There, while working together again, they found themselves in Dr. Bob's living room comparing notes. They discovered that between Akron, Cleveland, and New York there were forty "recovered" alcoholics. Suddenly it became apparent that the program was working, that there was hope. *Perhaps AA was working.*

Bill, ever the great entrepreneur, was filled with great visions. "Why, this is probably one of the greatest medical and spiritual developments of all time." Conceivably, AA could circle the earth. Bill visualized AA hospitals and hostels specializing in recovery. History was to see much of this vision realized. A major national poll as the program matured showed AA to be the eighty-eighth most important development of the century, as mentioned, and the number one most important spiritual development. Let us review the major events to this point leading Bill to his enthusiasm:

Summer 1934: Dr. Silkworth pronounces Bill W. a hopeless alcoholic.

August 1934: The Oxford Group sobers up Ebby T., a friend of Bill's.

November 1934: Ebby visits Bill and tells him his story.

December 1934: Bill's spiritual experience in the Charles Townes Hospital after which he never drank again. This became Bill's AA birthday.

December 1934 to May 7, 1935: Bill works with alcoholics, but fails to help any to sobriety.

May 12, 1935: Dr. Bob and Bill W. meet in Akron.

June 10, 1935: Dr. Bob has his last drink and AA is founded (although yet unnamed).

1937: The New York AA separates from the Oxford Group.

November 1937: Dr. Bob and Bill, meeting in Akron, become aware that there are now forty men sober and realize that success for AA is possible.

1939: The Akron and Cleveland groups leave the Oxford Group.

Success, however, was still in its earliest stages. The recovery circles began with the tiniest of arcs. The first meetings were held at Dr. Bob's home and were primarily Oxford Group meetings with an emphasis on recovery from alcoholism. As the meetings grew, great friends of the program T. Henry and Clarence Williams opened their homes and pocketbooks; they and others were Oxford Group members and were equally generous with their time, money, and homes. A great debt is owed to the Oxford Group of Akron and to these generous souls.

CHAPTER 72

FINANCIAL CONSIDERATIONS

With the separation from the Oxford Group, meeting places had to be rented and money was becoming an issue. Meeting places were not the only concern. Practical matters were beginning to become apparent. Members and volunteers were sustaining the groups out of their own pockets. One of the concepts being followed was that the program *should be cost free.* This was later incorporated into AA Tradition 7. Meeting rooms became necessary, and telephones were impossible to do without. Landlords found free rent an unacceptable practice, and utility and telephone companies had to be paid. *Cost free, a secret of sobriety.*

The program had to survive and a solution needed to be found. Alcoholics needed to be able to communicate with other alcoholics or they would remain ignorant of AA's fellowship and "suggestions." The cries of "let's *keep it simple"* had to come into balance with practical need. *Keep it simple, a secret of sobriety.*

Services AA could not perform itself were needed. Hospitalization and caring for the sick could not be the program's business (if they should be considered at all). Dr. Bob, Sister Ignatia, the Charles Townes Hospital, St. Thomas Hospital in Akron, Vincent Charity Hospital in Cleveland, the Knickerbocker Hospital in New York, and others came to the aid of the alcoholics in need of this type of care. *Singleness of purpose.*

CHAPTER 73

ALCOHOLICS ANONYMOUS IS BEGINNING TO BECOME KNOWN

Medicine, religion, industry, and the communications community began to become aware of the needs of the alcoholic and that Bill Wilson and Dr. Bob's program seemed to be an answer.

CHAPTER 74

FINANCIAL POSSIBILITIES

Continued progress brought sobering thoughts. How were the infant groups to provide for the basic needs of the group members? Must all alcoholics travel to Akron, Cleveland, or New York for help? To survive, AA needed answers. A strong possibility presented itself. Lois Wilson's brother, Dr. Leonard Strong, who had financed Bill's stays in the Charles Townes Hospital, was well known in New York. Dr. Strong's friends were among the most important social and financial figures in New York, one of whom was Willard Richardson.

JOHN D. ROCKEFELLER BECOMES INTERESTED

Mr. Richardson, a deeply religious man and the administrator of John D. Rockefeller Jr.'s private charities, became interested in the possibilities of AA. Through his influence, Mr. Rockefeller agreed to a meeting with the fledgling AA in his private boardroom. In attendance were Willard Richardson, Frank Amos, Leonard Strong, Bill Wilson, Dr. Bob, Dr. William Silkworth, and several members of the Akron and New York groups. Also present was Albert Scott, chairman of the board of trustees of Riverside Church, an entity Rockefeller used to administer his private charities. Mr. Scott became a strong advocate who called the AA effort a "living out of first century Christianity" (a reference to the growth of Christianity in the first through third centuries AD when Christianity was spread "person to person" as in AA as "alcoholic to alcoholic").

The meeting with John D. Rockefeller and associates began awkwardly, probably as the AA group was overcome by the wealth of those present. Finally, Willard Richardson, who had initially been attracted by the stories of the men's recovery, suggested the men begin by telling their stories. The meeting then began to go well. However, Bill's dream of hospitals and hostels did not materialize, as Rockefeller, influenced by Albert Scott, felt too much money would spoil the new program. Rockefeller and Scott feared money would create a professional class and spoil the "man to man" approach. At this juncture, Mr. Richardson described the desperate financial situation of Dr. Bob and Bill Wilson. Rockefeller did then put $5,000 into the Riverside Church account to be administered by the trustees of the church. *Singleness of purpose prevailed.*

Although Bill was bitterly disappointed, $5,000 in today's dollar would amount to nearly $90,000, a useful sum then or now. Charles Townes also contributed by loaning $2,500, about $45,000 today. He later loaned another $2,500. These sums were later paid back to Townes. The money issue, however, was not solved, and Mr. Amos, who was to become a good friend and longtime trustee for AA, promised to conduct an investigation of the society that might be a basis of asking Rockefeller for more funds. This never became necessary

CHAPTER 75

THE BOOK *ALCOHOLICS ANONYMOUS*

To raise money, a book was considered. A book could also present the AA program without an alcoholic being present, could reach those without group support, and could give cohesion to the present groups. The proceeds from the sale of the book, it was believed, could at least partially cover the financial needs of AA. After much controversy, the membership voted to commission Bill to write the book. The vote was not unanimous. Financially, the book was not the only consideration. It was believed the public would quickly realize AA was a viable solution to alcoholism. That support, unfortunately, was to be years coming.

WRITING THE BOOK BEGINS

With some of the financial pressure off, in May 1938, Bill began writing the book that was to become the *Big Book of Alcoholics Anonymous*. Bill was overwhelmed by the vastness of the project. He had no real experience in writing except technical and financial documents. He found he did not know how to begin a work of the scope contemplated.

Much of the material the group was considering for the book came from its previous association with the Oxford Group. Bill, considering the Oxford Group's principles as individualized by the new AA fellowship, realized the book should include these principles:

We admitted that we were licked, that we were powerless over alcohol (Step 1).

We made an inventory of our defects or sins (Step 4).

We confessed or shared our shortcomings with another person in confidence. (This, with the addition of sharing with God and a personal understanding of your own defects of character, became Step 5.)

We made restitution to all those we had harmed by our drinking (Step 9).

We tried to help other alcoholics with no thought of reward or prestige. (This includes much of the primary idea of Step 12.)

We prayed to whatever God we thought there was for the power to practice these ideals. (This became, essentially, Step 11).

Bill, Dr. Bob, and others had come to understand these values in stopping drinking. But could a newcomer see these ideas quickly enough for them to be useful without personal counseling? That was doubtful. These concepts are too complex and unclear unless you have studied the teaching of the Oxford Group, and too preachy and goody-goody for an alcoholic drinker to comprehend. *These six steps convey many of the original secrets of sobriety.*

HOW TO BEGIN

The impossibility of it all, even just starting the process, seemed to Bill daunting for a time. Bill then recalled that in the meeting with Rockefeller, inhibited by the wealth surrounding them, he and the others had difficulty communicating the needs of the fledgling association. He then remembered that Willard Richardson, sensing the problem, had said he first became interested in the program when he heard the stories of the recovering men.

Recalling this experience, Bill began by putting his own story on paper. This was to become chapter one. "There Is a Solution" became chapter two. After he had written each section, Bill sent his writing to Dr. Bob, to the Akron group, and to the Cleveland group—which had become quite large—and shared it with his New York group, seeking their ideas and contributions. Soon there were four chapters in draft form. It soon became apparent that there were widely different ideas concerning the book, although all were very enthusiastic that there should be a book.

Then, having arrived at chapter five, Bill and the alcoholics realized they had to state what the program was about and how it worked. This was to be the backbone of the book. Reconsidering everything he had learned in four years, Bill realized the program needed to be accurately and clearly stated so any prospective alcoholic reading the material would have an exact set of "steps" to follow. Even though he had a start, the necessity of describing how the process worked was in front of him.

Bill said the problem secretly worried the life out of him. He had never written anything of this stature, and neither had any of the other members of the group. There was little agreement concerning the first four **chapters**. Some days he felt like throwing the book out the window.

On the night he wrote the Twelve Steps of Alcoholics Anonymous, he was in a depression and not at all in a spiritual mood. He was exhausted and discouraged, but slowly his mind came into focus. He recalled AA until then had been strictly word of mouth using the basic ideas from the Oxford Group, from William James, from Dr. Silkworth, and from practical evolution. They included these key points:

We admitted that we were powerless over alcohol.

We got honest with ourselves.

We got honest with another person, in confidence.

We made amends for harms done others.

We worked with other alcoholics without demand for prestige or money.

We prayed to God to help us to do these things as best we could.

There was considerable variation on these ideas, though they stuck to the Oxford Group absolutes of honesty, purity, unselfishness, and love, although nothing was in writing. These principles were not definite enough, and to be compelling the literature would have to be as clear and comprehensible as possible. These steps would need to be explicit! There could be no loopholes new and rationalizing alcoholics could wiggle through. Perhaps the six ideas could be broken into smaller pieces and the spiritual implications of the presentation could be broadened.

PROGRESS

"Finally, I started to write. I set out to draft more than six steps, how many more I did not know. I relaxed and asked for guidance and with a speed that was astonishing I completed the first draft of the steps. It took perhaps half an hour. The words flew out. When I reached a stopping point, I numbered the new steps; there were twelve. Somehow this number seemed significant; I associated them with the twelve apostles. Perhaps for this reason I moved God into the second step, right up front. I named God liberally throughout the balance of the steps. In one step I suggested the newcomer get down on his knees."

THE BEGINNING OF THE CONCEPT OF A GROUP CONSCIENCE

When Bill W. showed the new documents to the New York meeting, the protests were loud and many. Atheist and agnostic friends did not go for the idea of kneeling. Others said the steps talked too much about God. Three points of views emerged: (1) A conservative group thought the book should be Christian in the doctrinal sense of the word. (2) A liberal group had no problem with the use of the word *God*, but insisted on no doctrinal basis such as Christianity. (3) Atheists and agnostics wanted God removed entirely and insisted the book should be purely psychological and medical.

Jim Burwell, an early New York member, emerged as the strongest advocate of the "no God" position, and his influence is credited with Bill editing the book and using the phrase "God as you understand Him" rather than simply "God." This phrase was in regular use by Sam Shoemaker. Without this change, the movement may not have survived. A more complete consideration of the "God Thing" will be discussed later. *God as you understand God, an important, perhaps critical, addition.* Bill finally got the group's permission to use his own judgment in order to finish the book. The steps as they survived were and are:

THE TWELVE STEPS OF ALCOHOLICS ANONYMOUS

1. Admitted we were powerless over alcohol—that our lives had become unmanageable.

2. Came to believe that a power greater than ourselves could restore us to sanity.

3. Decided to turn our will and our lives over to the care of God *as we understood Him.*

4. Made a searching and fearless moral inventory of ourselves.

5. Admitted to God, to ourselves, and to another human being the exact nature of our wrongs.

6. Were entirely ready to have God remove all these defects of character.

7. Humbly asked Him to remove our shortcomings.

8. Made a list of all persons we had harmed and became willing to make amends to them all.

9. Made direct amends to such people whenever possible, except when to do so would injure them or others.

10. Continued to take personal inventory and when we were wrong promptly admitted it.

11. Sought through prayer and meditation to improve our conscious contact with God, *as we understood Him*, praying only for knowledge of His will for us and the power to carry that out.

12. Having had a spiritual awakening as the result of these steps, we tried to carry this message to alcoholics, and to practice these principles in all our affairs.

CHAPTER 76

THE *BIG BOOK OF ALCOHOLICS ANONYMOUS*

The book was fleshing out. Bill's story became chapter one, "There Is a Solution," followed by chapter two, "More about Alcoholism"; chapter three, "We Agnostics"; chapter four, "How It Works"; chapter five, "Into Action"; chapter six, "Working with Others"; chapter seven, "To Wives"; chapter eight, "The Family Afterward"; chapter 9, "To Employers"; and chapter ten, "A Vision for You."

Bill concluded **chapter** eleven with these final two paragraphs: "Our book is meant to be suggestive only. We realize we know only a little. God will constantly disclose more to you and to us. Ask Him in your morning meditation what you can do each day for the man who is still sick. The answers will come if your own house is in order. But obviously you cannot transmit something you have not got. See to it that your relationship with Him is right, and great events will come to pass for you and countless others. This is the great fact.

"Abandon yourself to God as you understand God. Admit your faults to Him and to your fellows. Clear away the wreckage of the past. Give freely of what you find and join us. We shall be with you in the Fellowship of the Spirit, and you will surely meet some of us on the Road of Happy Destiny. May God bless and keep you—till then."

ADDITIONALLY

Before the chapters came a table of contents, preface, forewords to the various editions, and a doctor's opinion. The Twelve Steps were found on page 59 in "How It Works." After the first 164 pages came forty-two personal stories. The appendices covered the Twelve Traditions, spiritual experience, medical views on AA, the Lasker Award, religious views on AA, and how to get in touch with AA. The Twelve Steps appeared again in short form. This is the book as it was yet unpublished and unnamed.

A note of caution was raised: what if the book had medical errors or, equally serious, was offensive to some religious faith? As a precaution four hundred copies were sent out for evaluation. The reviews were positive.

CHAPTER 77

NAMING THE BOOK

Naming the book proved interesting. Bill had used the title *Alcoholics Anonymous* on the initial four hundred copies. But the three groups—New York, Akron, and Cleveland—found the title unacceptable. The New Yorkers had been calling themselves *A Nameless Bunch of Alcoholics*. Then *The One Hundred Men* became popular, then *The Way*. Everyone felt it was important to transmit hope, and so some favored the title *The Way Out*. Bill was tempted to call it *The Way Out: The B. W. Movement*. That title was slapped down, and Bill and the New Yorkers again began leaning toward *Alcoholics Anonymous*. Finally, the Library of Congress was consulted. *The Way* had been used thirteen times, *The Way Out* twenty-six. No one wanted to be thirteenth or twenty-sixth, so the name *Alcoholics Anonymous* became the name of the group or society. *We cannot imagine another name.*

CHAPTER 78

HOW TO PUBLISH THE BOOK

By the spring of 1938, a definite program of action took shape, and AA needed a tax-free charitable trust or foundation. Willard Richardson, Frank Amos, Leroy Chipman, and Dr. Strong agreed to act as trustees. The Alcoholic Foundation was thus established.

The next problem was how to finance the publication of the book. The Harper Publishing Company offered a $1,500 advance with normal royalties. Reader's Digest showed strong interest. One of the newest and most sober New Yorkers, Hank P., was an enthusiastic supporter of self-publishing; thus AA would own the book, possibly through the newly established Foundation.

Securing the funds for a book yet to be published, they were to discover, was a challenge. Those who knew the program were generally unable to afford an investment. Charles Townes had given the program $2,500, not as an investment, but as a loan. Later he loaned another $2,500. He was no longer a possibility.

Hank P. then conceived the plan of AA's own publishing company, a stock company. The new company was named Works Publishing Company. There were to be six hundred shares at a price of $25 per share. Two hundred shares were to be offered for sale and Bill and Hank would own four hundred.

Not one sale. The recovering community was generally financially challenged and had little disposable income. To make it easier the shares were then offered at $5 per month.

Hank and Bill reapproached Reader's Digest, which had shown positive interest in publishing a story. This piqued interest. Hank and Bill had also gone to Cornwell Publishing Company and arranged a down payment of only $500 to publish the book. The cost of publishing was to be less than $1 per book; at $3.50 per copy the profit would be particularly good. Works Publishing Company had to contract for five thousand copies.

Even $3.50 seemed expensive, so they chose the thickest paper available. The book was very thick and quickly got the nickname "The Big Book." The book was then printed but was warehoused until AA could pay Cornwall for the books. In 1939, AA, Word Publishing, Bill Wilson, Dr. Bob, and Hank P were broke. Reader's Digest had decided not to publish a story and there were five thousand books to pay for with no customers. Then fresh calamity hit: Bill and Lois's home was repossessed and sold. Everything they owned was in a warehouse and was to stay that way for two years. The situation was grim.

CHAPTER 79

EARLY STRUGGLES

Such was the state of AA, the book *Alcoholics Anonymous*, Bill and Lois Wilson and Dr. Bob and his wife, Anne, in the summer of 1939. All the drunks who had put up $4,500 were asking what had happened to the money. Charles Townes was also a little uneasy over the $5,000 he had loaned. What could they do? What would they do?

Charles Townes knew Morris Markey, a well-known writer. Markey was intrigued by what Townes had told him about AA, and he approached Fulton Oursler, the editor of *Liberty* magazine. *Liberty* had a religious orientation. Oursler saw the possibilities and agreed to publish an article. He later became a friend of Bill W.'s and served as a trustee of the Foundation.

WHAT HAPPENED

An AA member came to the rescue and loaned Bill and Lois their summer home. Another member loaned them a car. The AAs around New York passed the hat and were able to give Bill $50 a month for groceries. The future looked very dim, but Bill and the group began to shop around from one magazine to another for publicity. They found no takers. It looked like the whole program was going to come to an end.

Then, one of the more prosperous members, who had a fashionable clothing business on Fifth Avenue in New York City, appeared. The owner, Bert Taylor had his shop mortgaged to the hilt, having drunk most of its value up. Bill approached him and told him of a promised article upcoming with *Liberty* magazine. Bill may not have told him the article would not come out until September (if at all). He asked for $1,000 to carry them until the article was published. Bill told him the books would then go out in carloads. Bert said he did not have $1,000, but if Bill was sure about the article, he had a wealthy customer he could approach. Bert called and made the appeal but was asked for the financials on Works Publishing Company.

When Mr. Cochran examined the financials, he said sorry, but no thanks. Bert then asked if he would loan him the money personally, collateralized by his business. Mr. Cochran agreed. *Liberty* agreed to publish. Several stories followed in the *Cleveland Plain Dealer*. The $1,000 lasted until the *Liberty* article came out, and as a result eight hundred calls for help came in, resulting in enough sales for AA to squeak through 1939. The *Liberty* magazine article was religiously oriented and was titled "Alcoholics and God."

The article follows.

Is there hope for habitual drunkards?

A cure that borders on the miraculous—and it works!

For twenty-five or thirty cents we buy a glass of fluid which is pleasant to the taste, and which contains within its small measure a store of warmth and good-fellowship and stimulation, of release from momentary cares and anxieties. That would be a drink of whisky, of course—whisky, which is one of Nature's most generous gifts to man, and at the same time one of his most elusive problems. It is a problem because, like many of his greatest benefits, man does not quite know how to control it. Many experiments have been made, the most spectacular being the queer nightmare of prohibition, which left such deep scars upon the morals and the manners of our nation.

Millions of dollars have been spent by philanthropists and crusaders to spread the doctrine of temperance. In our time the most responsible of the distillers are urging us to use their wares sensibly, without excess.

But to a certain limited number of our countrymen neither prohibition nor wise admonishments have any meaning, because they are helpless when it comes to obeying them. I speak of the true alcoholics, and before going any further I had better explain what that term means.

For a medical definition of the term, I quote an eminent doctor who, has spent twenty-five years treating such people in a highly regarded hospital: "We believe ... that the action of alcohol in chronic alcoholics is a manifestation of an allergy—that the phenomenon of craving is limited to this class and never occurs in the average temperate drinker. These allergic types can never safely use alcohol in any form at all."

"They are," he goes on, "touched with physical and mental quirks which prevent them from controlling their own actions. They suffer from what some doctors call a 'compulsion neurosis.' They know liquor is bad for them but periodically, they are driven by a violent and totally uncontrollable desire for a drink. And after that first drink, the deluge."

Now these people are genuinely sick. The liquor habit with them is not a vice. It is a specific illness of body and mind and should be treated as such.

By far the most successful cure is that used by the hospital. It is, fundamentally, a process of dehydration: of whose doctor I have quoted. There is nothing secret about it. It has the endorsement of the medical profession. It is, fundamentally, a process of dehydration: of removing harmful toxins from all parts of the body faster than nature could accomplish it.

Within five or six days—two weeks at the maximum—the patient's body is utterly free from alcoholic poisons. Which means that the physical cravings are completely cured, because the body cries out for alcohol only when alcohol is already there. The patient has no feelings of revulsion toward whisky. He is simply not interested in it. He has recovered. But wait. How permanent is his recovery?

Our doctor says this: "Though the aggregate of full recoveries through physical and psychiatric efforts is considerable, we doctors must admit that we have made little impression upon the problem as a whole. For there are many types which do not respond to the psychological approach.

"I do not believe that true alcoholism is entirely a matter of individual mental control. I have had many men who had, for example, worked for a period of months on some business deal which was to be settled on a certain date ...

"For reasons for which they could not afterward explain, they took a drink a day or two prior to the date ... and the important engagement was not even kept. These men were not drinking to escape. They were drinking to overcome a craving beyond their mental control.

"The classification of alcoholics is most difficult. There are, of course, the psychopaths who are emotionally unstable ... They are over remorseful and make many resolutions—but never a decision.

"There is the type who is unwilling to admit that he cannot take a drink just like the rest of the boys. He does tricks with his drinking—changing the brand, or only drinking after meals or changing his companions. None of this helps him strengthen his control and be like other people. There are types entirely normal in every respect except in the effect which alcohol has upon them ...

"All these, and many others, have one symptom in common. They cannot start drinking without developing the phenomenon of craving ...The only relief we have to suggest is complete abstinence from alcohol.

"But are these unfortunate people really capable, mentally, of abstaining completely? Their bodies may be cured of craving. Can their minds be cured? Can they be rid of the deadly compulsion neurosis?"

Among physicians the general opinion seems to be that chronic alcoholics are doomed. But wait!

Within the last four years, evidence has appeared which has startled hardboiled medical men by proving that this compulsive neurosis can be entirely eliminated. Perhaps you are one of those cynical people who will turn away when I say that the root of this new discovery is religion. But be patient for a moment. About three years ago a man appeared at the hospital in New York of which our doctor is head physician. It was his third cure.

Since his first visit he had lost his job, his health, his friends, and his self-respect. He was now living on the earnings of his wife.

He had tried every method he could find to cure his disease: had read all the great philosophers and psychologists. He had tried religion but he simply could not accept it. It would not seem real and personal to him.

He went through the cure as usual and came out of it in low spirits. He was lying in bed, emptied of vitality and thought, when suddenly, a strange and totally unexpected thrill went through his body and mind. He called out for the doctor. When the doctor came in, the man looked up at him and grinned.

"Well, Doc," he said, "my troubles are over. I've got religion."

"Why, you're the last man … "

"Sure, I know all that. But I have got it. And I know I'm cured of this drinking business for good." He talked with great intensity for a while and then said, "Listen, Doc. I've got to see some other patient—one that is about to be dismissed."

The doctor demurred. It all sounded a trifle fanatical. But finally consented. And thus was born the movement which is now flourishing with almost sensational success, Alcoholics Anonymous.

Here is how it works:

Every member of the group—which is every person who has been saved— is under obligation to carry on the work, to save other men.

That, indeed, is a fundamental part of his own mental cure. He gains strength and confidence by active work with other victims.

He finds his subject among acquaintances, at a "cure" institution or perhaps by making inquiry of a preacher, a priest, or a doctor. He begins his talk with his new acquaintance by telling him the true nature of his disease and how remote are his chances for permanent cure.

When he has convinced the man he is a true alcoholic and must never drink again, he continues:

"You had better admit that this thing is beyond your own control. You have tried to solve it by yourself, and you have failed. All right. Why not put this thing in the hands of Somebody Else?"

Even though the man might be an atheist or an agnostic, he will almost always admit that there is some sort of force operating in the world—some cosmic power weaving a design. And his new friend will say: I do not care what you call this Somebody Else. We call it God. But whatever you want to call it, you had better put yourself into its hands. Just admit you are licked, and say, "Here I am, Somebody Else. Take care of this thing for me."

The new subject will generally consent to attend one of the weekly meetings of the movement.

He will find twenty-five or thirty ex-drunks gathered in somebody's home for a pleasant evening. There are no sermons. The talk is gay or serious as the mood strikes. The new candidate cannot avoid saying to himself, "These birds are ex-drunks. And look at them! They must have something. It sounds kind of screwy, but whatever it is I wish to heaven I could get it too." One or another of the other members keeps working on him day by day. And presently the miracle. But let me give you an example: I sat down in a quiet room with Mr. B., a stockily built man of fifty with a rather stern, intelligent face.

"I'll tell you what happened a year ago," he said. I was completely washed up. Financially I was all right because my money is in a trust fund. But I was a drunken bum of the worst sort. My family was almost crazy with my incessant sprees.

"I took the cure in New York. (At the hospital we have mentioned.)

"When I came out of it, the doctor suggested I go to one of those meetings the boys were holding. I just laughed. My father was an atheist and had taught me to be one. But the doctor kept saying it would not do me any harm, and I went.

"I sat around and listened to the jabber. It did not register with me at all. I went home. But the next week I found myself drawn to the meeting. And again, they worked on me while I shook my head. I said, 'It seems O.K. with you, boys, but I don't even know your language. Count me out.'

"Somebody said the Lord's Prayer, and the meeting broke up. I walked three blocks to the subway station. Just as I was about to go down the stairs—bang!" He snapped his fingers hard. "It happened! I do not like that word miracle, but that is all I can call it. The lights in the street seemed to flare up. My feet seemed to leave the pavement. A kind of shiver went over me, and I burst out crying.

"I went back to the house where we had met, and rang the bell, and Bill let me in. We talked until two o'clock in the morning. I haven't touched a drop since, and I've set four other fellows on the same road."

The doctor, a nonreligious man himself, was at first utterly astonished at the result that began to appear among his patients. But then he put his knowledge of psychiatry and psychology to work. These men were experiencing a psychic change. Their so-called "compulsion neurosis" was being altered—transferred from liquor to something else. Their psychological necessity to drink was being changed to a psychological necessity to rescue their fellow victims from the plight that made them so miserable. It is not a new idea. It is a powerful and effective working out of an old idea. We all know the alcoholic has an urge to share his troubles.

Psychoanalysts use this urge. They say to the alcoholic in basic terms: "You can't lick this problem yourself. Give me the problem—transfer the whole thing to me and let me take the whole responsibility."

But the psychoanalyst, being of human clay, is not often a big enough man for that job. The patient simply cannot generate enough confidence in him. But the patient can have enough confidence in God—once he has gone through the mystical experience of recognizing God. And upon that principle the Alcoholic Foundation rests.

The medical profession, in general, accepts the principle as sound.

"Alcoholics Anonymous" have consolidated their activities in an organization called the Alcoholic Foundation. It is a non-profit-making enterprise. Nobody connected with it is paid a penny. It is not a crusading movement.

It condemns neither liquor nor the liquor industry. Its whole concern is with the rescue of allergic alcoholics, the small proportion of the population who must be cured or perish. It preaches no particular religion and has no dogma, no rules. Every man conceives God according to his own lights.

Groups have grown up in other cities. The affairs of the Foundation are managed by three members of the movement and four prominent business and professional men, not alcoholics, who volunteered their services.

The Foundation has recently published a book, called *Alcoholics Anonymous*. And if alcoholism is a problem in your family or among friends, I heartily recommend that you get hold of a copy. It may very well help you to guide a sick man—an allergic alcoholic—on the way to health and contentment.

CHAPTER 80

THE JOHN D. ROCKEFELLER DINNER

In all this time AA had heard nothing from John D. Rockefeller, when all of a sudden, in February 1940, Mr. Richardson came to a trustee meeting of the Foundation and announced he had great news: Mr. Rockefeller, who had followed AA's progress with interest, wanted to give the fellowship a dinner. He would invite his friends to see the beginning of this new and promising start of AA. John D. was ill and could not attend, so his son Nelson conducted the meeting and concluded the dinner by announcing that AA was a work that proceeded on goodwill and needed no money. After the dinner, the $2 billion he represented got up and left.

That was a tremendous letdown, but AA was not let down for too long. After the dinner, Mr. Rockefeller asked that the talks and pamphlets be printed, and he bought four hundred books to send to his friends along with a personal letter to each of them. "They need little or no money," he said, "but I am giving them $1,000."

Alcoholics Anonymous received $3,000 as a result of the letters, and about $3,000 a year for the next five years. The publicity AA received from the dinner brought in book orders and AA was finally able to pay its secretary.

CHAPTER 81

JACK ALEXANDER'S *SATURDAY EVENING POST* ARTICLE

Without doubt, the single most important financial event came in March 1941. Jack Alexander wrote a terrific article in the *Saturday Evening Post* about AA. The article brought in about seven thousand inquiries. I secured a copy. It was amazing. Jack Anderson was a skeptic assigned to investigate the infant AA program to determine if there was a story there. Anderson spent months conducting the investigation, traveling all over the east and Midwest. In order to explain the program from the view of a skeptical professional, I include his article.

JACK ALEXANDER'S ARTICLE ON ALCOHOL ANONYMOUS

MARCH 1, 1941

Jack Alexander was assigned to report on the fledgling AA program. He was very resistant as he believed alcoholics simply choose to drink and alcoholism is merely poor character with a lack of integrity. Nevertheless, the *Post* insisted, and Jack spent months examining the program and its participants. His attitude began to change, he grew enthusiastic about the assignment, and he did a first-class job of reporting. These are his findings.

INTRODUCTION

Alcoholics Anonymous had its beginnings in 1935 when a doctor and a layman, both alcoholics, helped each other recover and then developed, with a third recovering alcoholic, the organization's guiding principles. By 1941, the group had demonstrated greater success in helping alcoholics than any previous methods and had grown to about two thousand members. But for most of North America, AA was still unknown. Following the March 1, 1941, publication of an article in the *Saturday Evening Post* describing AA's extraordinary success, inquiries began to flood in, leaving the small staff of what was then a makeshift headquarters overwhelmed. Alcoholics Anonymous tripled in size in the next year and continued to grow exponentially. Today, AA claims 2 million members worldwide and 1.2 million in the United States. Following is the original *Post* article many credit for AA's success.

THE ARTICLE

Three men sat around the bed of an alcoholic patient in the psychopathic ward of Philadelphia General Hospital one afternoon a few weeks ago. The man in the bed, who was a complete stranger to them, had the drawn and slightly stupid look that inebriates get while being defogged after a bender. The only thing noteworthy about the callers, except for the obvious contrast between their well-groomed appearances and that of the patient, was the fact that each had been through the defogging process many times himself. They were members of Alcoholics Anonymous, a band of ex-problem drinkers who make an avocation of helping other alcoholics to beat the liquor habit.

The man in the room was a mechanic. His visitors had been educated at Princeton, Yale, and Pennsylvania and were, by occupation, a salesman, a lawyer, and a publicity man. Less than a year before, one had been in shackles in the same ward. One of his companions had been what is known among alcoholics as a sanatorium commuter. He had moved from place to place, bedeviling the staffs of the country's leading institutions for the treatment of alcoholics. The other had spent twenty years of his life, all outside institution walls, making life miserable for himself, his family, and his employers, as well as sundry well-meaning relatives who had the temerity to intervene.

The air of the ward was thick with the aroma of paraldehyde, an unpleasant smelling mixture of alcohol and ether, which hospitals sometimes use to taper off the paralyzed drinker and soothe his squirming nerves. The visitors seemed oblivious of this and the depressing atmosphere that clings to even the nicest of psychopathic wards. They smoked and talked with the patient for twenty minutes or so, then left their personal cards and departed. If the man in the bed felt he would like to see one of them again, they told him, he had only put in a telephone call.

They made it plain that if he actually wanted to stop drinking, they would leave their work or get up in the middle of the night to hurry to where he was. If he did not choose to call, that would be the end of it. The members of Alcoholics Anonymous do not pursue or coddle a malingering prospect and they know the strange tricks of the alcoholic as a reformed swindler knows the art of bamboozling.

Herein lies much of the unique strength of a movement which, in the past six years, has brought recovery to about 2,000 men and women, a large percentage of whom had been considered medically hopeless. Doctors and clergymen, working separately or together, have always managed to salvage a few cases. In isolated instances, drinkers have found their own method of quitting. But inroads into alcoholism have been negligible and it remains one of the great unsolved public health enigmas.

By nature touchy and suspicious, the alcoholic likes to be left alone to work out his puzzle, and he has a convenient way of ignoring the tragedy which he inflicts meanwhile upon those who are close to him. He holds desperately to a conviction that, although he has not been able to handle alcohol in the past, he will ultimately succeed in becoming a controlled drinker. One of medicine's queerest animals, he is, as often as not, an acutely intelligent person. He fences with professional men and relatives who attempt to aid him, and he gets a perverse satisfaction out of tripping them up in argument.

There is no specious excuse for drinking which the troubleshooters of Alcoholics Anonymous have not heard or used themselves. This upsets him a little and he gets defensive. He looks at their neat clothing and smoothly shaved faces and charges them with being goody-goodies who do not know what it is to struggle with drink. They reply with relating their own stories—the double Scotches and brandies breakfast; the vague feeling of discomfort which precedes a drinking bout, the awakening from a spree without being able to account for the actions of several days and the haunting fear that possibly they had run down someone with their automobiles.

They tell of the eight-ounce bottles of gin hidden behind pictures and in caches from cellar to attic; of spending whole days in motion-picture houses to stave off the temptation to drink; of sneaking out of the office for quickies during the day. They talk of losing jobs and stealing money from their wives' purses; of putting pepper into whisky to give it a tang; of tippling on bitters and sedative tablets, or on mouthwash or hair tonic; of getting into the habit of camping outside the neighborhood tavern ten minutes before opening time. They describe a hand so jittery that it could not lift a pony to the lips without spilling the contents; of drinking liquor from a beer stein because it can be steadied with two hands, although at the risk of chipping a front tooth; of tying an end of a towel about a glass, looping the towel around the back of the neck and drawing the free end with the other hand, pulley fashion, to advance the glass to the mouth; of hands so shaky they feel as if they were about to snap off and fly into space; of sitting on hands for hours to keep them from doing this.

These and other bits of drinking lore usually manage to convince the alcoholic that he is talking to blood brothers. A bridge of confidence is thereby erected, spanning a gap that has baffled the physician, the minister, the priest, or the hapless relatives. Over this connection, the troubleshooters convey, bit by bit, the details of a program for living which has worked for them and which, they feel, can work for any other alcoholic. They concede as out of their orbit only those who are psychotic or who are already suffering from the physical impairment know as wet brain. At the same time, they see to it that the prospect gets whatever medical attention is needed.

Many doctors and staffs of institutions throughout the country now suggest Alcoholics Anonymous to their drinking patients. In some towns the courts and probation officers co-operate with the local group. In a few city psychopathic divisions, the workers of Alcoholics Anonymous are accorded the same visiting privileges as staff members. Philadelphia General is one of those. Dr. John F. Stouffer, the chief psychiatrist, says: The alcoholics we get here are mostly those who cannot afford treatment, and this is by far the greatest thing we have ever been able to offer them. Even those who occasionally land back in here again we observe a profound change in personality, You would hardly recognize them.

The *Illinois Medical Journal*, in an editorial last December, went further than Dr. Stouffer, stating: It is indeed a miracle when a person who for years has been more or less constantly under the influence of alcohol and in whom his friends have lost all confidence, will sit up all night with a "drunk" and at stated intervals administer a small amount of liquor in accordance with a doctor's order without taking a drop himself."

This is a reference to a common aspect of the Arabian Night adventures to which Alcoholics Anonymous workers dedicate themselves. Often it involves sitting upon, as well as up with, the intoxicated person, as the impulse to jump out a window seems to be an attractive one to many alcoholics when in their cups. Only an alcoholic can squat on another alcoholic's chest for hours with the proper combination of discipline and sympathy.

During a recent trip around the East and Middle West I met and talked with scores of A.A.s, as they call themselves, and found them to be unusually calm, tolerant people. Somehow, they seemed better integrated than the average group of nonalcoholic individuals. Their transformation from cop fighters, canned heat drinkers and, in some instances, wife beaters, was startling. On one of the most influential newspapers in the country I found that the city editor, the assistant city editor, and a nationally known reporter were A.A.s, and strong in the confidence of their publisher.

In another city I heard a judge parole a drunken driver to an A.A. member. The latter, during his drinking days, had smashed several cars and had had his own operator's license suspended. The judge knew him and was glad to trust him. A brilliant executive of an advertising firm disclosed that two years ago he had been panhandling and sleeping in a doorway under an elevated structure. He had a favorite doorway which he shared with other vagrants, and every few weeks he goes back and pays them a visit just to ensure himself he is not dreaming. In Akron, as in other manufacturing centers, the groups include a heavy element of manual workers. In the Cleveland Athletic Club, I had lunch with five lawyers, an accountant, an engineer, three salesmen, an insurance man, a buyer, a bartender, a chain store manager, a manager of an independent store and a manufacturer's representative. They were members of a central committee which coordinates the work of nine neighborhood groups. Cleveland, with more than 450 members, is the biggest of A.A. centers. The next largest are located in Chicago, Akron, Philadelphia, Los Angeles, Washington, and New York. All told there are groups in about 50 cities and towns.

SELF-INSURANCE AGAINST DEMON RUM

In discussing their work, the A.A.'\s spoke of their drunk rescuing as "insurance" for themselves. Experience within the group has shown, they said, that once a recovered drinker slows up in this work, he or she is likely to go back to drinking himself. There is, they agreed, no such thing as an ex-alcoholic. If one is an alcoholic—that is, a person who is unable to drink normally—one remains an alcoholic until he dies, just as a diabetic remains a diabetic. The best he can hope for is to become an arrested case, with drunk saving as his insulin. At least, the A.A.s say so, and medical opinion tends to support them. All but a few said that they had lost all desire for alcohol. Most serve alcohol in their homes when friends drop in and they still go to bars with companions who drink. The A.A.s tipple on soft drinks and coffee.

One, a sales manager, acts as bartender at his company's annual jamboree in Atlantic City and spends his nights tucking the celebrators into their beds. Only a few of those who recover fail to lose the feeling that at any minute they may thoughtlessly take one drink and skyrocket off on a disastrous binge. An A.A. who is a clerk in an Eastern city has not had a snifter in three and a half years but says that he still has to walk fast past saloons to circumvent the old impulse; but he is an exception. The only hangover from the wild days that plague the A.A. is a recurrent nightmare. In the dream, he finds himself off on a rousing whooper-dooper, frantically trying to conceal his condition from the community. Even this symptom disappears shortly, in most cases. Surprisingly, the rate of employment among these people, who formerly drank themselves out of job after job, is said to be around 90 per cent.

One-hundred-percent effectiveness with non-psychotic drinkers who sincerely want to quit is claimed by the workers of Alcoholics Anonymous. The program will not work, they add, with those who only "want to want to quit," or want to quit because they are afraid of losing their families or their jobs. The effective desire, they state, must be based on enlightened self-interest; the applicant must want to get away from liquor to head off incarceration or premature death. He must be fed up with the stark social loneliness which engulfs the uncontrolled drinker, and he must want to put some order into his bungled life.

As it is impossible to disqualify all borderline applicants, the working percentage of recovery falls below the 100 per cent mark. According to A.A. estimation, 50 per cent of the alcoholics taken in hand recover almost immediately; 25 percent get well after suffering a relapse or two, and the rest remain doubtful. This rate of success is exceptionally high. Statistics on traditional medical and religious cures are lacking, but it has been informally estimated that they are no more than 2 or 3 percent effective on run-of-the-mill cases.

Although it is too early to state that Alcoholics Anonymous is the definitive answer to alcoholism, its brief record is impressive, and it is receiving hopeful support. John D. Rockefeller, Jr., helped defray the expenses of getting it started and has gone out of his way to get other prominent men interested.

Rockefeller's gift was a small one, in deference to the insistence of the originators that the movement be kept on a voluntary basis. There are no salaried organizers, no dues, no officers, and no central control. Locally, the rents of assembly halls are met by passing the hat at meetings. In small communities no collections are taken, as the gatherings are held in private homes. A small office in downtown New York acts merely as a clearing house for information. There is no name on the door and mail is received anonymously through Box 658, Church Street Annex post office. The only income, which is money received from the sale of a book describing the work, is handled by the Alcoholic Foundation, a board composed of three alcoholics and four non-alcoholics.

In Chicago 25 doctors work hand in hand with Alcoholics Anonymous contributing their services and referring their own alcoholic patients to the group, which now numbers around 200. The same co-operation exists in Cleveland and to a lesser degree in other centers. A physician, Dr. W. D. Silkworth, of New York City, gave the meeting its first encouragement. However, many doctors remain skeptical. Dr. Foster Kennedy, an eminent New York neurologist, probably had these in mind when he stated at a meeting a year ago: "The aim of those concerned in this effort against alcoholism is high, their success rate has been considerable, and I believe medical men of good will should aid."

The active help of two medical men of good will, Drs. A. Wiese Hammer and C. Dudley Saul, has assisted greatly in making the Philadelphia unit one of the more effective of the younger groups. The movement there had its beginning in an offhand way in February 1940, when a businessman who was an A.A. convert was transferred to Philadelphia from New York. Fearful of backsliding for lack of rescue work, the newcomer rounded up three bar flies and started to work on them. He got them dry and the quartet began ferreting out other cases. By last December 15, 99 alcoholics had joined up. Of these 86 were now total abstainers—39 from one to three months, and 25 from six to ten months. Five who had joined the unit after having belonged in other cites had been nondrinkers from one to three years.

At the other end of the time scale, Akron, which cradled the movement, holds the intramural record for sustained abstinence. According to a recent check-up, two members have been riding the A.A. wagon for five and a half years, one for five years, three for four and a half years, one for the same period with one skid, one for two and a half years, and 13 for two years. Previously, most of the Akronites and Philadelphians had been unable to stay away from liquor for longer than a few weeks.

In the Middle West, the work had been almost exclusively among persons who have not arrived at the institutional stage. The New York group, which has a similar nucleus, makes a sideline specialty of committed cases, and has achieved striking results. In the summer of 1939, the group began working on the alcoholics confined in Rockland State Hospital, at Orangeburg, a vast mental sanitarium which gets the hopeless alcoholic backwash of the big population centers. With the encouragement of Dr. R. E. Blaisdell, the medical superintendent, a unit was formed within the walls and meetings were held in the recreation hall. New York A.A.s went to Orangeburg to give talks and on Sunday evenings the patients were brought in state-owned busses to a clubhouse which the Manhattan group rents on the West Side.

Last July first, eleven months later, records kept at the hospital showed that of 54 patients released to Alcoholics Anonymous, 17 had no relapse and 14 others had had only one. Of the rest, nine had gone back to drinking in their home communities, 12 had returned to the hospital and two had not been traced. Doctor Blaisdell has written favorably about the work to the State Department of Mental Hygiene, and he praised it officially in his last annual report.

Even better results were obtained in two public institutions in New Jersey, Greystone Park and Overbrook, which attracts patients of better economic and social backgrounds than Rockland, because of their nearness to prosperous suburban villages. Of seven patients released from the Greystone Park Institution in two years, five have abstained for periods of one to two years, according to A.A. records. Eight of ten released from Overbrook have abstained for about the same length of time. The others have had from one to two relapses.

Why people become alcoholic is a question on which authorities disagree. Few think that anyone is "born an alcoholic." One may be born, they say, with a hereditary predisposition to alcoholism, just as one may be born with a vulnerability to tuberculosis. The rest seems to depend upon environment and experience, although one theory has it that some people are allergic to alcohol, as hay-fever sufferers are to pollens. Only one note is found to be common to all alcoholics, emotional immaturity. Closely related to this is an observation that an unusually large number of alcoholics start out in life as an only child, as a youngest child, or as the only boy in a family of girls or as the only girl in a family of boys. Many have records of childhood precocity and were what were known as spoiled children.

Frequently the situation is complicated by an off-center home atmosphere in which one parent is unduly cruel, the other overindulgent. Any combination of these factors, plus a divorce or two, tends to produce neurotic children who are poorly equipped emotionally to face the ordinary realities of adult life. In seeking escapes, one may immerse himself in his business, working twelve to fifteen hours a day, or in sports or in some artistic sideline. Another finds what he thinks is a pleasant escape in drink. It bolsters his opinion of himself and temporarily wipes away any feeling of social inferiority which he may have. Light drinking leads to heavy drinking. Friends and family are alienated, and employers become disgusted. The drinker smolders with resentment and wallows in self-pity. He indulges in childish rationalizations to justify his drinking—he has been working hard and he deserves to relax, his throat hurts from an old tonsillectomy and a drink would ease the pain, he has a headache, his wife does not understand him, his nerves are jumpy, everybody is against him, and so on. He unconsciously becomes a chronic excuse maker for himself.

All the time he is drinking he tells himself, and those who butt into his affairs, that he can really become a controlled drinker if he wants to. To demonstrate his strength of will, he goes for weeks without taking a drop. He makes a point of calling at his favorite bar at a certain time each day and ostentatiously sipping milk or a carbonated beverage, not realizing he is indulging in juvenile exhibitionism. Falsely encouraged, he shifts to a routine of one beer a day, and that is the beginning of the end once more. Beer leads inevitably to more beer and then to hard liquor. Hard liquor leads to another first-rate bender. Oddly, the trigger which sets off the explosion is as apt to be a stroke of business success as it is to be a run of bad luck. An alcoholic can stand neither prosperity nor adversity.

CURING BY CATHARSIS

The victim is puzzled on coming out of the alcoholic fog. Without his being aware of any change, a habit had gradually become an obsession. After a while, he no longer needs his rationalization to justify the fatal first drink. All he knows is that he feels swamped by uneasiness or elation, and before he realizes what is happening, he is standing at a bar with an empty whisky pony in front of him and a stimulating sensation in his throat. By some peculiar quirk of his mind, he has been able to draw a curtain over the memory of the intense pain and remorse caused by preceding stem-winders. After many experiences of this kind, the alcoholic begins to realize that he does not understand himself; he wonders whether his power of will, though strong in other fields, is not defenseless against alcohol. He may go on trying to defeat his obsession and wind up in a sanitarium. He may give up the fight as hopeless and try to kill himself. Or he may seek outside help.

If he applies to Alcoholics Anonymous, he is first brought around to admit that alcohol has him whipped and that his life has become unmanageable. Having achieved this state of intellectual humility, he is given a dose of religion in its broadest sense. He is asked to believe in a power greater than himself, or at least to keep an open mind on that subject while he goes on with the rest of the program. Any concept of the higher power is acceptable. A skeptic or agnostic may choose to think of his inner self, the miracle of growth, a tree, man's wonderment at the physical universe, the structure of the atom or mere mathematical infinity. Whatever form is visualized, the neophyte is taught that he must rely on it and, in his own way, to pray to the power for strength.

He next makes a sort of moral inventory of himself with the private aid of another person—one of his AA sponsors, a priest, a minister, a psychiatrist, or anyone else he fancies. If it gives him any relief, he may get up at a meeting and recite his misdeeds, but he is not required to do so. He restores what he may have stolen while intoxicated and arranges to pay off old debts and to make good on rubber checks: he makes amends to persons he has abused and, in general, cleans up his past as well as he is able to. It is not uncommon for his sponsors to lend him money to help out in the early stages.

This catharsis is regarded as important because of the compulsion which a feeling of guilt exerts in the alcoholic obsession. As nothing tends to push an alcoholic toward the bottle more than personal resentments, the pupil also makes out a list of his grudges and resolves not to be stirred by them. At this point he is ready to start working on other alcoholics. By the process of extroversion, which the work entails, he is enabled to think less of his own troubles.

The more drinkers he swings into Alcoholics Anonymous, the greater his responsibility to the group becomes. He cannot get drunk now without injuring the people who have proved themselves his best friends. He is beginning to grow up emotionally and to quit being a leaner. If raised in an orthodox church he usually, but not always, become a regular communicant again.

Simultaneously with the making over of the alcoholic goes the process of adjusting his family to his new way of living. The wife or husband of an alcoholic, and the children too, frequently become neurotics from being exposed to drinking excesses over a period of years. Re-education of the family is an essential part of a follow-up program which has been devised.

Alcoholics Anonymous, which is a synthesis of old ideas rather than a new discovery, owes its existence to the collaboration of a New York stockbroker and an Akron physician. Both alcoholics, they met for the first time a little less than six years ago. In 35 years of periodic drinking, Doctor Armstrong, to give the physician a fictitious name, had drunk himself out of most of his practice. Armstrong had everything, including the Oxford Group, and had shown no improvement. On Mother's Day, 1935, he staggered home, in typical drunk fashion, lugging an expensive potted plant, which he placed on his wife's lap. Then he went upstairs and passed out.

At that moment, nervously pacing the lobby of an Akron hotel, was the broker from New York, whom we shall arbitrarily call Griffith. Griffith was in a jam. In an attempt to obtain control of a company and rebuild his financial fences, he had come out to Akron and engaged in a fight for proxies. He had lost the fight. His hotel bill was unpaid. He was almost flat broke. Griffith wanted a drink.

During his career in Wall Street, Griffith had turned some sizeable deals and had prospered, but, through ill-timed drinking bouts, had lost out on his main chances. Five months before coming to Akron he had gone on the water wagon, through the ministrations of the Oxford Group in New York. Fascinated by the problem of alcoholism, he had gone back as a visitor to a Central Park West detoxicating hospital, where he had been a patient, and talked to the inmates. He effected no recoveries but found that by working on other alcoholics he could stave off his own cravings.

A DOCTOR FOR A PATIENT

A stranger in Akron, Griffith knew no alcoholics with whom he could wrestle. A church directory, which hung in the lobby opposite the bar, gave him an idea. He telephoned one of the clergymen listed and through him got in touch with a member of the local Oxford Group. This person was a friend of Armstrong's and was able to introduce the physician and the broker at dinner. In this manner Doctor Armstrong became Griffiths' first real disciple. He was a shaky one, at first. After a few weeks of abstinence, he went East to a medical convention and came home in a liquid state. Griffith, who had stayed in Akron to iron out some legal tangles arising from the proxy battle, talked him back to sobriety. That was on June 10, 1935. The nips the physician took were the last drinks he was to ever take.

Griffith's lawsuits dragged on, holding him over in Akron for six months. He moved his baggage to the Armstrong home, and together the pair struggled with other alcoholics Before Griffith went back to New York, two more Akron converts had been obtained. Meanwhile, both Griffith and Dr. Armstrong had withdrawn from the Oxford Group, because they felt that its aggrieve evangelism and some of its other methods were hindrances in working with alcoholics. They put their own techniques on a strict take-it-or-leave-it basis and kept it there.

Progress was slow. After Griffith had returned east, Doctor Armstrong and his wife, a Wellesley graduate, converted their home into a free refuge for alcoholics and an experimental laboratory for the study of the guests' behavior. One of their guests, who, unknown to the hosts, was a manic depressive as well as an alcoholic, ran wild one night with a kitchen knife. He was overcome before he stabbed anyone. After a year and a half, a total of ten persons had responded to the program and were abstaining. What was left of the family savings had gone into the work. The physician's new sobriety caused a revival in his practice, but not enough of one to carry the extra expense. The Armstrongs, nevertheless, carried on, on borrowed money, Griffith, who had a Spartan wife, too, turned his Brooklyn home into a duplicate of the Akron menage. Mrs. Griffith, a member of an old Brooklyn family, took a job in a department store and in her spare time played nurse to inebriates. The Griffiths also borrowed, and Griffith managed to make odd bits of money around the brokerage house. By the spring of 1939, the Armstrongs and the Griffiths had between them cozened about one hundred alcoholics into sobriety.

In a book which they published at that time the recovered drinkers described the cure program and related their personal stories. The title was *Alcoholics Anonymous*. It was adopted as a name for the movement itself, which up to that time had none. As the book got into circulation, the movement spread rapidly.

Today Doctor Armstrong is still struggling to patch up his practice. The going is hard. He is in debt because of his contributions to the movement and the time he devotes gratis to alcoholics. Being a pivotal man in the group, he is unable to turn down the requests for help which flood his office.

Griffith is even deeper in the hole. For the past two years he and his wife have had no home in the ordinary sense of the word. In a manner reminiscent of the primitive Christians, they have moved about, finding shelter in the homes of A.A. colleagues, and sometimes wearing borrowed clothing.

A SELF-STARTING MOVEMENT

Having got something started, both movers want to retire to the fringes of their movement and spend more time getting back on their feet financially. They feel that the way the thing is set up it is virtually self-operating and self-multiplying. Because of the absence of figureheads and the fact that there is no formal body of belief to promote, they have no fear that Alcoholics Anonymous will degenerate into a cult.

The self-starting nature of the movement is apparent from letters in the files of the New York office. Many persons have written in saying that they stopped drinking as soon as they read the book and made their homes meeting places for small chapters. Even a fairly large unit, in Little Rock, got started in this way. An Akron civil engineer and his wife, in gratitude for his cure four years ago, have been steadily taking alcoholics into their home. Out of thirty-five such wards, thirty-one have recovered.

Twenty pilgrims from Cleveland caught the idea in Akron and returned home to start a group of their own. From Cleveland, by various means, the movement has spread to Chicago, Detroit, St. Louis, Los Angeles, Indianapolis, Atlanta, San Francisco, Evansville, and other cities. An alcoholic newspaperman with a surgically collapsed lung moved to Houston for his health. He got a job on a Houston paper and through a series of articles which he wrote for it started an A.A. unit which now has thirty-five members. One Houston member has moved to Miami and is now laboring to snare some of the most eminent winter colony lushes. A Cleveland traveling salesman is responsible for starting small units in many parts of the country. Fewer than half of the A.A. members have ever seen Griffith or Doctor Armstrong.

Even to an outsider who is mystified, as most of us are, by the antics of problem drinkers, the results which have been achieved are amazing. This is especially true of the most virulent cases, a few of which are herewith sketched under names that are not their own.

Sarah Martin was a product of the F. Scott Fitzgerald era. Born of wealthy parents in a Western city, she went to Eastern boarding schools and "finishing" in France. After making her debut, she married. Sarah spent her nights drinking and dancing until daylight. She was known as a girl who could carry a lot of liquor. Her husband had a weak stomach, and she became disgusted with him. They were quickly divorced. After her father's fortune had been erased in 1929, Sarah got a job in New York and supported herself. In 1932, seeking adventure, she went to Paris to live and set up a business of her own, which was successful. She continued to drink heavily and stayed drunk longer than usual. After a spree in 1933 she was informed that she had tried to throw herself out a window. During another bout she did jump or fall—she does not remember which—out of a first-floor window. She landed on her face on the sidewalk and was laid up for six months of bone setting, dental work, and plastic surgery.

In 1936 Sarah Martin decided that if she changed her environment by returning to the United States, she would be able to drink normally. This childish faith in geological change is a classic delusion which all alcoholics get at one time or another. She was drunk all the way home on the boat. New York frightened her and she drank to escape it. Her money ran out and she borrowed from friends. When her friends cut her, she hung around Third Avenue bars caging drinks from strangers. Up to this point, she had diagnosed her troubles as a nervous breakdown. Not until she had committed herself to several sanatoriums did she realize she was an alcoholic. On advice of a staff doctor, she got in touch with an Alcoholic Anonymous group. Today she has another good job and spends many of her nights sitting on hysterical women drinkers to prevent them from diving out of windows. In her late thirties, Sarah Martin is an attractively serene woman. The Paris surgeons did handsomely by her.

Watkins is a shipping clerk in a factory. Injured in an elevator mishap in 1927, he was furloughed with pay by a company that was thankful he did not sue for damages. Having nothing to do during a long convalescence, Watkins loafed in speak-easies. Formerly a moderate drinker, he started to go on drunks lasting several months. His furniture went for debts and his wife fled, taking their three children. In eleven years, Watkins was arrested twelve times and served eight workhouse sentences. Once, in an attack of delirium tremens, he circulated a rumor among the prisoners that the county was poisoning the food in order to reduce the workhouse population and save expenses. A mess-hall riot resulted. In another fit of DTS, during which he thought the man in the cell above was trying to pour hot lead on him, Watkins slashed his own wrists and throat with a razor blade. While recuperating in an outside hospital, with eighty-six stitches, he swore never to drink again. He was drunk before the final bandages were removed. Two years ago, a former drinking companion got him into Alcoholics Anonymous and he has not touched liquor since. His wife and children have returned, and his home has new furniture. Back at work, Watkins has paid off a major part of $2,000 in debts and petty alcoholic thefts and has his eye on a new automobile.

At twenty-two, Tracy, a precocious son of well-to-do parents, was credit manager for an investment banking firm whose name has become a symbol of the money-mad 20s. After the firm's collapse during the stock-market crash, he went into advertising and worked up to a post which paid him $23,000 a year. On the day his son was born Tracy was fired. Instead of appearing in Boston to close a big advertising contract, he had gone on a spree and had wound up in Chicago, losing out on the contract. Always a heavy drinker, Tracy became a bum. He tippled on canned heat and hair tonic and begged from cops, who are always easy touches for amounts up to a dime. On one sleety night Tracy sold his shoes to buy a drink, putting on a pair of rubbers he had found in a doorway and stuffing them with paper to keep his feet warm.

THE CONVIVIAL A.A.s

He started committing himself to sanitariums, more to get out of the cold than anything else. In one institution, a physician got him interested in the

A.A. program. As part of it, Tracy, a Catholic, made a general confession and returned to the church, which he had long since abandoned. He skidded back to alcohol a few times but after a relapse in February 1939, Tracy took no more drinks. He has since then beat his way up again to $28,000 a year in advertising.

Victor Hugo would have delighted in Brewster, an adventurer who took life the hard way. Brewster was a lumberjack, cowhand, and wartime aviator. During the postwar era he took up flask-toting and was soon doing a cook's tour of the sanitariums. In one of them, after hearing about shock cures, he bribed the Negro attendant in the morgue with gifts of cigarettes to permit him to drop in each afternoon and meditate over a cadaver. The plan worked well until the day he came on a dead man who, by a freak of facial contortion, wore what looked like a grin. Brewster met up with the A.A.s in December 1938, and after achieving abstinence got a job which involved much walking. Meanwhile, he had got cataracts on both eyes. One was removed, giving him distance sight with the aid of thick-lens spectacles. He used the other eye for close-up vision, keeping it dilated with an eye-drop solution in order to avoid being run down in traffic. Then he developed a swollen, or milk, leg. With these disabilities, Brewster tramped the street for six months before he caught up with his drawing account. Today, at age fifty, and still hampered by his physical handicaps, he is making his calls and is earning around $400 a month.

For the Brewsters, the Martins, the Watkins, the Tracys and the other reformed alcoholics, congenial company is now available wherever they happen to be. In the larger cities A.A.s meet one another daily at lunch in favored restaurants. The Cleveland groups give big parties on New Year's and other holidays, at which gallons of coffee and soft drinks are consumed. Chicago holds open house on Fridays, Saturdays, and Sunday—alternately, on the North, West, and South Sides—so that no lonesome A.A. need revert to liquor over the weekend for lack of companionship. Some play cribbage or bridge, the winner of each hand contributing to a kitty for paying off entertainment expenses. The others listen to the radio, dance, eat, or just talk. All alcoholics, drunk or sober, like to gab. They are among the most society-loving people in the world, which may help to understand why they got to be alcoholics in the first place.

I have included this article by Jack Alexander in order to give you the feel of the AA program in its early days. The national exposure of the program no doubt gave the program a huge shot in the arm and certainly exposed the opportunity of sobriety to many years before it had previously been possible.

The article obscured the true identities of Bill Wilson and Dr. Bob Smith for the sake of anonymity. Since, however, their true selves are well known, and both are deceased, identification is approved by AA. I have personally not identified with the program as a member as the program requests that a personal relapse not reflect on the program. My regard for the program, however, is high.

To further your understanding of Jack Alexander's growing regard for AA I include the process of his growth in perception and his earlier skepticism and low regard. I include his thoughts as he recalls his earlier perceptions of four years earlier.

It began when the *Post* asked me to look into A.A. as a possible article subject. All I knew of alcoholism at that time was that, like most other non-alcoholics, I had had my hand bitten (and my nose punched) on numerous occasions by alcoholic pals to whom I had extended a hand—unwisely, it always seemed afterward. Anyway, I had an understandable skepticism about the whole business.

My first contact with actual A.A.s came when a group of four of them called at my apartment one afternoon. Each one introduced himself as an alcoholic who had gone dry: as the official expression has it. They were good-looking and well dressed, and as we sat around drinking Coca Colas (which was all they would take), they spun yarns about their horrendous drinking misadventures. The stories sounded spurious, and after the visitors had left, I had a strong suspicion that my leg was being pulled. They had behaved like a bunch of actors sent out by some Broadway casting agency.

Ordinarily, diabetes is not rated as one of the hazards of reporting, but the Alcoholics Anonymous article in the *Saturday Evening Post* came close to costing me my liver, and maybe A.A. neophytes ought to be told this when they are handed copies of that article to read. It might impress them. In the course of my fact gathering, I drank enough Coca-Cola, Pepsi-Cola, ginger ale, Moxie and Sweetie to float the Saratoga. Then there was the thickly frosted cake so beloved of A.A. gatherings, and the heavily sweetened coffee, and the candy. Nobody can tell me that alcoholism is not due solely to an abnormal craving for sugar, not even a learned psychiatrist. Otherwise, the AA assignment was a pleasure.[1]

After my meeting with the A.A. group, I took the subway to the headquarters of Alcohol Anonymous in downtown Manhattan where I met Bill W. This Bill W is a very disarming guy and an expert at indoctrinating the stranger into the psychology, psychiatry, physiology, pharmacology, and folklore of alcoholism. He spent the good part of a couple of days telling me what it was all about. It was an interesting experience, but at the end of it my fingers were still crossed, without my saying it, and in the days that followed he took me to the homes of some of the A.A.s, where I got a chance to talk to the wives, too. My skepticism suffered a few minor scratches, but not enough to hurt. Then Bill shepherded me to a few A.A. meetings at a clubhouse somewhere in the West Twenties. Here all manner of alcoholics, many of them, the nibblers at the fringe of the movement, still fragrant of liquor and needing a shave. Now I knew I was among a few genuine alcoholics anyway. The bearded, fume-breathing lads were A.A. skeptics, too, and now I had some company.

The week spent with Bill W was a success from one standpoint. I knew I had the makings of a readable report but, unfortunately, I did not quite

---

1   Author's note: Abusive alcohol consumption causes a dopamine imbalance in the brain. When alcohol use is stopped, mood changes occur which result in the brain seeking rebalance by seeking another source—in this case, sugar.

believe in it and told Bill so. He asked why I did not look in on the A.A.s in other cities and see what went on there.

I agreed to do this, and we mapped out an itinerary. I went to Philadelphia first, and some of the local A.A.s took me to the psychotic ward of Philadelphia General Hospital and showed me how they work on the alcoholic inmates. In that gloomy place, it was an impressive thing to see men who had bounced in and out of the ward themselves patiently jawing a man who was still haggard and shaking from a binge that wound up in the gutter.

Akron was the next stop. Bill met me there and promptly introduced me to Doc S. who is another hard man to disbelieve. There were more hospital visits, an A.A. meeting, and interviews with people who a year or two before were undergoing varying forms of the blind staggers. Now they seemed calm, well-spoken, steady-handed, and prosperous, at least mildly prosperous.

Doc S drove us from Akron to Cleveland one night and the same pattern was repeated. The universality of alcoholism was more apparent here, In Akron it had been mostly factory workers. In Cleveland there were lawyers, accountants, and other professional men, in addition to laborers. And again, the same stories. The pattern was repeated also in Chicago, the only variation there being the presence at the meetings of a number of newspapermen. I had spent most of my working life on newspapers and I could really talk to these men. The real clincher, though, came in St. Louis, which is my hometown. Here I met a number of my own friends who were A.A.s, and the last remnants of skepticism vanished. Once rollicking rum pots, they were now sober. It did not seem possible, but there it was.

When the article was published, the reader-mail was astonishing. Most of it came from desperate drinkers, or their wives, or from mothers, fathers, or interested friends. The letters were forwarded to the A.A. office in New York and from there were sent on to A.A. groups nearest to the writer of the letter. I do not know exactly how many letters came in, all told, but the last time I checked, a year or so ago, it was about 6,000. They still trickle in from time to time, from people who have had the article in pockets all this time or kept in the bureau drawer under the handkerchief case intending to do something about it.

I guess the letters will keep coming in for years, and I hope they do, because now I know that every one of them springs from a mind, either of an alcoholic or of someone close to him, which is undergoing a type of hell that Dante would have gagged at. And I know, too, that this victim is on the way to recovery, if he wants to recover. There is something very heartening about this, particularly in a world which has been struggling toward peace for centuries without ever achieving it for exceptionally long periods of time.

CHAPTER 82

JACK ALEXANDER: FROM SKEPTIC TO BELIEVER

ALCOHOLICS ANONYMOUS: AN OVERNIGHT, SUCCESSFUL, NATIONAL INSTITUTION

Immediately after the article appeared, more than six thousand letters arrived, which were sent to AA and distributed to the local groups. Alcoholics Anonymous became a national institution overnight, and the AA book became a success. Today the book has sold more than 30 million copies and was placed on the *Times* list of the one hundred best and most influential books written in English since 1923. The Library of Congress designated it as one of the books "Books That Shaped America". The second edition was published in 1955, the third edition in 1976, the fourth edition in 2001. The *Big Book* has been translated into almost every language.

CHAPTER 83

IMPORTANT DATES

In 1938, Bill and Dr. Bob organized a trusteeship for the growing membership with the cooperation of friends of John D. Rockefeller. In 1939, the *Cleveland Plain Dealer* carried a series about AA that included positive editorials. Thereafter the twenty members of the Cleveland group were deluged by countless calls for help. There was no time for new members to get indoctrinated in AA before they were pressed into service. Soon Cleveland's membership swelled to five hundred. For the first time it was demonstrated AA could grow quickly. In the fall of 1939, an article in *Liberty* magazine, as previously reported, resulted in eight hundred urgent calls for help.

In 1940, the Rockefeller dinner resulted in $1,000 from Rockefeller and $3,000 from his friends, and additionally $3,000 a year for five years, also as previously noted. That event generated a lot of positive publicity. At the close of 1940, membership stood at two thousand.

Then, in March 1941, a seminal event took place: Jack Anderson's article in the *Saturday Evening Post* was published, garnering more than seven thousand replies, book sales, and the membership jumping to six thousand. Alcoholics Anonymous spread across the United States and Canada as the fellowship mushroomed.

The period from 1940 to 1950, although the membership grew to more than one hundred worldwide, was a time of great uncertainty. The issue was how to create an environment where mercurial alcoholics could live and work together. How could a system be created that would allow such a disparity of personalities and thinking to coexist for the greater good? These issues were the principal occupation of the New York headquarters during this period. Correspondence with thousands of groups developed sound conclusions that would suit AA's purpose. Those conclusions became the Twelve Traditions of AA. These were codified by 1946, and by 1950, the earlier chaos was largely a thing of the past.

In 1950, the First International Convention was held in Cleveland. There Dr. Bob made his last appearance. He died on November 16, 1950. But before he died, as reported, he and the remarkable Sister Ignatia had cared for five thousand sufferers at St. Thomas Catholic Hospital. Sister Ignatia continued the work until many more sufferers were cared for and brought to AA. The example of medicine and religion working in concert was firmly established at Cleveland's Charity Hospital and other hospitals around the nation. (See Jack Anderson's *Saturday Evening Post* article for a complete list of hospitals he visited during his investigation.)

The Twelve Traditions, first written in 1946, were confirmed at the convention. They had been reduced from the old "long form" to capsule statements, which in form more closely match the Twelve Steps of Recovery. The Twelve Traditions were to become the platform of unity and function on which the fellowship would henceforth stand. This platform has since become known as "the steps" to direct the meetings.

CHAPTER 84

ALCOHOLICS ANONYMOUS'S STEPS IN MATURITY

These dates were important milestones, and the New York office began to greatly expand its activities. There was now an office of public relations, another for advising new groups, and other offices that served hospitals, prisons, those away from other meetings, and those in other countries, as well as other offices too numerous to mention.

PUBLISHING

The headquarters were now publishing AA literature and translating the book, pamphlets, and other literature into the language of each country. The "Grapevine" had achieved a large circulation. These and other activities were becoming increasingly indispensable to AA.

A BOARD OF TRUSTEES

More importantly, all these activities were in the hands of a board of trustees. Previously the only administrative link to AA had been Dr. Bob and Bill W. Dr. Bob's death brought the matter to a head. It had become necessary to link AA's trusteeship, which had become the General Service Board of Alcoholics Anonymous, with the fellowship it served. The fellowship could not be allowed to die with Bill W.

THE CONFERENCE

Therefore, the decision was reached to have a conference with two delegates from each state with the provision that states with heavy populations could have extra delegates. The first meeting took place in April 1951 and included only the US and Canada delegates. The delegates would be in two panels elected in alternate years to avoid total turnover every year. This temporary scheme became known as the "Third Legacy." This plan was put into fifty thousand pamphlets and sent to all the AA groups known to national headquarters in order to fully inform the new delegates of suggested itineraries before they arrived in New York.

The new delegates arrived in New York and were introduced to all the facets of AA headquarters. The conference has been held each April since and has been named the General Service Conference. Alcoholics Anonymous had come of age.

THE GENERAL SERVICE CONFERENCE

The General Service Conference Charter promise to AA:

In all its proceedings, the General Service Conference shall observe the spirit of the AA Traditions, taking great care that the Conference never becomes the seat of wealth or power; that sufficient operating funds, plus an ample reserve, be its prudent financial principle; that none of the Conference members shall ever be placed in a position of unqualified authority over any of the others; that all important decisions be reached by discussion, vote and, whenever possible, by substantial unanimity; that no Conference action shall ever be personally punitive or an incitement to public controversy; that though the Conference may act for the service of Alcoholics Anonymous, it shall never perform any acts of government; and that, like the society of Alcoholics Anonymous which it serves, the Conference itself will always remain democratic in thoughts and action.

ALCOHOLICS ANONYMOUS AFTER TWENTY YEARS

In 1955, AA celebrated its twentieth anniversary at its convention in St. Louis. The second edition of *Alcoholics Anonymous* was published. Alcoholics Anonymous was on its way.

CHAPTER 85

AS ALCOHOLICS ANONYMOUS GREW, SO GREW THE AUTHOR

THE AUTHOR IN 1955

I was twenty and on my way to needing the AA program. My father was forty-three and never found it. The disease took its toll on him eighteen years later; he was sixty-one. I was headed in the same direction. I was beginning to drink alcoholically although not yet as seriously as it was to become. It would be thirty years before I would reach the AA program I have described.

CHAPTER 86

BECOMING ALCOHOLIC

People can become alcoholics in enumerable ways: some claim to be born that way. I believe, from research, that an individual with one parent who is alcoholic has a better than 50 percent chance of becoming an alcoholic; if both parents are alcoholic, the odds reach 80 percent plus. Recall I said a chance. These figures are remembered, hopefully correctly, from my studies in obtaining a degree in alcohol and drug counseling. These statistics are reinforced by figures from internet sources that show children with alcoholic parents are four times as likely to face becoming alcoholic, females less so than males. Others can cross the line into alcoholism from drinking too heavily and for too long—the list goes on.

Most alcoholics enter AA when they hit a "bottom." This occurs when the price of drinking becomes too dear—the human price, that is. A "low bottom drunk" will have lost his house, his job, his wife and family, his health, many of his friends, and often his life. Sometimes he ends up on the street. This is the alcoholic envisioned by the general public: the man on the street with a brown paper bag containing a bottle of cheap wine. Of course, many of these street people are dually addicted and mentally ill to some degree. On the street are a variety of alcoholics, many unwilling to trade the freedom of living on the street for the more confining, in their view, lifestyle of recovery. Each of these alcoholics fiercely defends his or her brand of alcoholism. The "beer alcoholics" will tell you they are not winos, "that wine never saw a grape." The more well-to-do alcoholics, or those on the way down, generally choose vodka; some, however incorrectly, think vodka cannot be smelled on the breath.

CHAPTER 87

EARLY ALCOHOLISM

In the beginning, however, there were only "low bottom" drunks in AA. Of the first one hundred recovering men (and one woman), each one had lost everything. Most had been in asylums and hospitals several times. Of the first one hundred mentioned in the foreword of the original edition of *Alcoholics Anonymous*, probably more than half had relapsed more than once.

Very slowly, alcoholics, who had not fallen to the depths to which the first one hundred had, began to find sobriety. That "bottom" kept rising until today there are those who enter the "program" at the earliest sign of addiction to alcohol. This is due to multiple factors. The military and industry began realizing the cost of alcoholism, and now have programs for when alcohol shows signs of interfering with the lives and efficiency of the services, the companies, or their members. The court system was getting strict with those involved in auto accidents and family violence. Recovery programs were becoming an alternative to incarceration for judges.

HIGH BOTTOMS

Alcoholism and addiction, however, were beginning to lose their stigma. Families and workplaces were using interventions to prevent alcoholism's progress. It was no longer unusual for an abuser of alcohol to self-initiate into a program such as AA or into a formal program that usually then sends it clients to AA.

The high bottom drunk has not lost his house, is still working at his job, and is still married. He or she may be about to lose their house, their job, and their marriage may be on the rocks, but not over just yet. Interventions from family and work may intercede, and recovery may begin; often, they may have had a "nudge from the judge," a term for when a judge gives the option of jail or AA upon a conviction for a DUI (driving under the influence) or other event involving the abuse of alcohol. Occasionally, a friend already in AA may have influenced the alcoholic toward recovery.

Seldom will an alcoholic try to quit drinking on his own, which is quite different than attempting sobriety through AA. These attempts are usually unsuccessful. Usually a "promise" to quit drinking is merely an attempt to get out of the immediate situation with no real intention to stop drinking. There are a variety of recoveries in between these general classifications.

EARLY RECOVERY

My story is of the more or less high bottom variety, but my wife and family have paid a high price. I had no idea I had a disease, that my style of drinking to excess could be a disease. I had never heard of AA. I believed, occasionally, I should moderate my drinking, strongly influenced by Ginny's attitude about our drinking. Ginny was ready for sobriety, or at least a more normal life. I was merely doing what I believed it took to get out of my present predicament or to reduce my stress level.

I was in complete denial concerning my alcoholism, or perhaps unaware of it. I thought that the relaxing aspect of drinking was keeping my stress level down so I would not have a heart attack. I was also completely unaware how dangerous was a blood pressure of 250 over 150 (my memory) and a pulse twice normal. I had just been told by my doctors at age forty-nine I had less than a year to live, yet I had not connected my poor health with my drinking.

Ginny and I drank together for more than seventeen years. I have mentioned we met on the rebound from our failed marriages. Drinking eased the pain of what we may have considered our failure in our marriages, and we drank together every day. In retrospect, I probably influenced Ginny to drink and then faced her with a lifestyle that she may have believed was relieved by alcohol.

Whatever the facts may have been, we raised a family in a very dysfunctional home. My oldest daughter, Cindy, became a serious addict by age eleven. Her younger sister, Allison, was becoming an alcoholic and possibly an addict; Jack Daniels was her drink, as to whether she took drugs I was unaware. My son said she used, especially marijuana. Allison died in a boating accident at age nineteen. As we were still drinking, I immediately allowed myself to jump more seriously into the bottle. It crossed my mind that now no one would blame me for drinking. Allison was just starting college to become a nurse.

Their older brother Rusty, my first son, was injured, also in a boating accident, at age six and later died by drowning. Of my children with Ginny, my oldest son was a serious crystal methamphetamine addict and later added other drugs and alcohol. Our daughter was an addict and later an alcoholic. She had at one time a blood alcohol level of over .400. She died in her early forties of physical issues and complications of the disease. She had, however, fourteen years clean and sober in AA. Only our second son was not addicted to alcohol or drugs, but he was of course affected by the family disease. Our oldest son and daughter have been in recovery in the AA program.

CHAPTER 88

A NEW DYNAMIC IN THE FAMILY

Recovery from the disease of alcoholism created a totally new family dynamic. The AA program began a new phase in our life. During this time, I was challenged by a neighbor to go to church with them. I was the atheist on the block, and I habitually made fun of their attempts to interest me in church. Finally, I gave in to their constant challenge and went to church with them on a dare, probably to get them off my back.

It was a Baptist church whose minister, Tim LaHaye, was a very prominent pastor, an author of eighty-five books, and the president of a Christian school and Christian Heritage College. The first time I attended church with my neighbors, I was very embarrassed to experience an urgent altar call and a long walk from high in the balcony to the pastor at the altar.

I could not explain it, but it led to over three years of not drinking.

Be aware I termed it, "not drinking," not "sobriety." As members of the church, for about three years, we had good years. We did not drink during those years, but we were not sober as we know sobriety today in AA. I finally drank again, and Ginny joined me. The Christian phase was over for now. Soon we were drinking as obsessively as before. When we got sober again in 1986, Ginny began attending church without me. It was years into the program before I rejoined Ginny in church.

I began to take the AA program increasingly seriously. Ginny, however, took to the program with even greater enthusiasm and volunteered for every service opportunity, read everything available, and left me far behind in the program of recovery. Ginny had an immediate acceptance of all aspects of the program and mine was to be of the educational variety— that is, sobriety came much more slowly to me until the *empirical* facts of the success of the program became impossible to ignore. *Empirical: Relying on experience or observation alone, often without or regard for system or theory.*

CHAPTER 89

THE PROMISES

The AA program made us several promises:

If we are painstaking about this phase of our development, we will be amazed before we are halfway through. We are going to know a new freedom and a new happiness. We will not regret the past nor wish to shut the door on it. We will comprehend the word *serenity* and we will know peace. No matter how far down the scale we have gone, we will see how our experience can benefit others. That feeling of uselessness will disappear. We will lose interest in selfish things and gain interest in our fellows. Self-seeking will slip away. Our whole attitude and outlook on life will change. Fear of people and economic security will leave us. We will instinctively know how to handle situations which used to baffle us. We will suddenly realize that God is doing for us what we could not do for ourselves.

Are these extravagant promises? We think not. They are being fulfilled among us sometimes quickly, sometimes slowly. They will always materialize if we work for them.

These promises are found on pages 83 and 84 of *Alcoholics Anonymous*.

CHAPTER 90

THE NEXT YEARS

We were to find these promises were to come true for us, never quickly, slowly, but come true they have. We slowly worked our way out of my alcoholism debt, although it took seven years.

I did not become "wonderful" the day I quit drinking, nor did Ginny. Most of our alcoholic habits were overcome with time. My reputation improved, but very slowly. I learned people have long memories and recalled I had promised to stop drinking a hundred times or more. People initially believed it was merely another promise to be broken. I had to re-earn a respectable reputation. It was now several years into sobriety. It was about 1989. I was about fifty-three.

I was still traveling to Taiwan on business and buying and selling yachts, although Taiwanese yachts were now becoming much too expensive to successfully merchandise. I had begun traveling to London, Tunisia, Guatemala, and the South Pacific, still obsessed with "big deals" and hitting a financial home run.

Ginny believed I would never make another penny and went back to college. She had a successful college career and graduated in 1992 with a bachelor's degree in social work and in 1994 with a master's degree, also in social work. She had interned during this time and contributed much of our family income.

Ginny inherited our home from her father, and we began an extensive remodel in about 1996. For the next year, I was involved in the remodeling of the one-hundred-year-old Craftsman home while maintaining its integrity. It still had gas light connections and knob and tube wiring. The oak flooring was original, and Ginny kept the home original but with modern appliances and features. We spent more than $200,000 on the remodel; the home eventually was appraised for more than $1 million. I got Ginny to mortgage the home to the limit and did honest but foolish projects in a down economy. With a refinance, our payments reached $6,000 per month.

CHAPTER 91

SHADOW VALLEY MINING COMPANY

I was now fully involved in the Shadow Valley Mining Company. I drove there each Monday morning from San Diego, about 275 miles. At the site we had two trailer houses and our tools; we had no electricity, and everything was very manual. My partner Bill N.'s two brothers were partners along with a Texan who had invested $100,000. We had no salaries to meet, only expenses for food and gas. The Texan was not with us often, so we were four workers. I chose to be the cook as I was excused from labor an hour before each meal. Learning to make gravy was a process. I was an awful cook for a while, but I am now more competent. Slowly we made progress and gradually bought equipment enough to become functional. Our assay results were quite good, and that somehow became known in the industry.

CHAPTER 92

MONTANA MINING COMPANY

We were approached by a mining firm in Montana whose mine had become financially unprofitable, we were told, when the price of gold dropped below $800 per ounce, too low for them to continue mining at a profit. They however, had millions of dollars' worth of equipment and were able to invest $40,000 per month. They become major partners, although we retained controlling interest of the corporation. All seemed well. Soon trucks began arriving with everything we needed to become fully functional.

Shadow Valley Mining Company was now becoming fully operational. We built an excellent laboratory, living quarters for a working crew, a home for the on-site working partner, Bill N., and his family, living quarters and an efficient galley for a cook, and a garage for a handyman and his wife. We had our own well for water complete with gravity flow to all the buildings. We had our own electrical generating plant. We were totally self-sufficient.

Our laboratory was equipped with a carbon arc spectrograph purchased from the City of Los Angeles. The original cost was $125,000, but we purchased it used for $25,000. The spectrograph would create a temperature of 10,000 degrees centigrade and would burn ore, creating a spectrograph. We would then compare the spectrograph to charts of known ores. Each element has a different spectrum and identification occurs instantly, making a portion of the process of assaying ore quick and accurate.

Another very high-tech device in our laboratory was an atomic absorption machine. These spectro-analytical procedures were for quantitative and qualitative determination of an ore. We could determine what the ore was and its concentration. This enabled us to quickly determine the areas in which to spend our efforts. We had probably $500,000 of chemicals in the lab, all purchased from a bankruptcy for much less. We had super sensitive scales. We had several ovens capable of temperatures high enough to melt metals out of ore samples. In other words, we were a first-rate laboratory on an excellent property and capable of our own assays.

Our machinery included equipment for digging the ore from the ground, a rock crusher to reduce the ore to a workable size, and other equipment to further pulverize the ore to a size where chemicals can more easily act on the metals and get it into solution. We had our own cement plant and three cement trucks. Commercial cement plants were too far away for the cement to be delivered: it would harden before arriving. We had a giant crane, with a boom over six stories high, highly capable to erect three tanks sixty feet high, each with a twenty-foot diameter. These huge tanks allowed the chemicals to slowly react with the crushed ore in quantity. Another tank, thirty feet tall with an eight-foot diameter, had a grinder at the bottom to reduce the material to a size appropriate for chemicals to surround the ore particles. There were earthmovers, including a bulldozer, a backhoe, and a front loader large enough to pick up a Volkswagen. There was a water truck, other trucks, and much more. We had a license for explosives. We were self-reliant and operational.

CHAPTER 93

THE REAL MONTANA MINING COMPANY

A shadow came over the horizon—the monthly investment stopped coming, and we discovered an amazing story. Montana Mining, although an existing mining company, existed as a company through which they laundered money from a large drug operation. They had misjudged our integrity and felt we would be a perfect fit. Perhaps our previous reputations influenced their choice. They were well regarded in Montana as the president was a high elected official. For reasons of liability, I will not mention his name or position, but he was one of the top five elected officials in the state. They were busted, and regrettably we were included in the indictment due to our business relationship. Our president had to stand trial with the Montana group. He spent considerable time in Montana during the trial. Happily, we were fully acquitted, and all the Montana Mining Company personnel were sent to prison on long terms.

We soon were fully back in operation and had competing companies building adjacent to our properties. Their values were much less than ours. After several years, we had an offer of $50,000,000 for a tiny percentage of Shadow Valley Mining Company.

Shadow Valley Mining Company was on Bureau of Land Management (BLM) property. When someone has a claim on BLM property and does a prescribed amount of work on the property each year, the BLM will deed the property to the claimant. We had far exceeded the necessary financial requirement and could have at any time had the property deeded to Shadow Valley Mining Company. There was no time requirement in having the property deeded to Shadow Valley Mining Company. We elected to lease the land during the construction to complete the building phase of the property, and therefore elected to temporarily lease as Federal OSHA was much less strict than Cal OSHA.

CHAPTER 94

WE WERE DENIED HAVING THE PROPERTY DEEDED TO SHADOW VALLEY MINING COMPANY

This proved to be a serious error. When we applied for a new permit to include the new buyer, we were refused. The BLM believed we were not a legitimate operation, no doubt influenced by the recent legal process we were involved in with the Montana Mining Company. Also, we later learned an employee we had terminated had spread the story, in a coffee shop frequented by members of the BLM, that we were a drug lab.

Drug labs generally cost only several thousand dollars to build and operate, while we had just received an audited financial of more than $7,000,000, as we were in the process of taking the company public. To take a company public requires an audited financial by a certified public accounting firm licensed to provide such a financial. The property has to be appraised, including each individual piece of equipment and each building. The anticipated value of the entire project is also considered.

CHAPTER 95

THE BLM'S INVASION OF SHADOW VALLEY MINING COMPANY

Nevertheless, the BLM took the story seriously as drug labs were common in the desert, due probably to the remoteness of the area. On a Saturday morning, a crew of twelve trucks and a helicopter arrived on the property with a full complement of engineers and inspectors. To avoid embarrassment, we speculate, upon finding Shadow Valley Mining Company was a serious mining operation, they did a complete inspection of the property. They had a backhoe dig 278 holes on the property. They found one infraction: a battery left on the ground improperly. During this "inspection," they discovered our explosives. Without checking that we were properly licensed, they decided to explode them. Their "explosives expert" was a social worker the year before and had limited experience with explosives. As a result, they set off the explosives too near the buildings. The explosion was so severe it knocked the helicopter out of the sky and so seriously damaged the buildings they became unusable. The chemicals in the laboratory were blown off the shelves and created a dangerously toxic purple chemical cloud.

The BLM, to justify its action, did not allow us back on the property for nearly a year. In that time, nearly all the equipment was stolen—caterpillars, loaders, digging equipment, trucks, everything. Shadow Valley Mining Company became a name with no assets.

CHAPTER 96

SUING THE US GOVERNMENT

We, of course, immediately sued the BLM. The first day of discovery, the government sent so many attorneys to the first lawsuit meeting we had to pay more than $500 merely to provide enough copies of the lawsuit for each attorney. The lawsuit took sixty-one months to settle; we won, but we were awarded less than $1 million.

We had lost a $50,000,000 contract, all our equipment, four large buildings including a fully equipped laboratory with expensive equipment as described, and five years of our lives.

A word to the wise—do not sue the government. Bill N. was so discouraged he and his family left California for South Carolina and bought a farm. I returned to the yacht business.

CHAPTER 97

GEORGIA AND SOUTH CAROLINA BUSINESSES

After Bill recovered his spirit, which took several years, he began a construction company in Augusta, Georgia. He became successful and bought a large property in Augusta for his operation. He rented much of the property to a car rental company and a national modular home sales company. He had become self-sufficient and successful.

During his success, he found an opportunity to buy an apartment complex with land enough to build two hundred condominiums in Hilton Head, South Carolina. We had remained friends and he called and asked me to partner in the project. Of course my job was the raise the millions necessary to purchase the property and build the units. The property's large apartment complex was several years old, but fully rented. The corporation was in Chapter 7 bankruptcy in a Washington DC federal court due to misuse of funds.

I first had to attend the bankruptcy hearing and make an offer on the property. I was successful in those efforts. I then was able to arrange financing, millions, with a Manhattan bank. These efforts took months and deadlines were important as the property would go to the highest bidder if I were not successful to meet our obligation with the federal bankruptcy court on the appropriate date.

All our plans were made. We had placed a large tentative order for the first section of condominiums and had completed engineering and permitting. I had purchased a home in Hilton Head to be near the work, which was expected to take several years. This was September 2001. On the 11th, Islamic terrorists flew several planes into the Twin Towers in New York: a day that will live in infamy. Our bank was below the towers and among those destroyed. As a result, we were not able to fund our obligation with the bankruptcy court in Washington, DC, within the prescribed time limit. The ensuing depression would have made it difficult to sell two hundred condominiums, so this was a mixed blessing: millions in profit versus a difficult process.

CHAPTER 98

MY FIRST STORAGE COMPANY

Bill N. was much more financially involved and was ruined. He had borrowed $30,000 from me and to pay it back he deeded the Augusta property to me. The property was more than ten acres on a major intersection in Augusta. The mortgage payments were more than $5,000 a month. The rental income was about $6,000 a month, so I was in no trouble. I had become friends with the holder of the mortgage, a very well-known and respected man from Augusta. He is, or was, the membership chairman for Augusta National, probably the most famous golf course in the world. He was the chairman of the board of our Augusta Sun Trust Bank, a valuable friend and partner regrettably now deceased.

Several things happened, probably a result of the depressed market due to 9/11: the auto rental company, Federal Rent-A-Car, decided to close the Augusta store. I decided to buy it rather than lose the income. This was to become an enormous mistake. I had to pay $20,000 for the franchise and buy the entire inventory from a huge auction company owned by Cox Cable. The cost was more than $300,000. Cox Cable was a difficult creditor, and my payments were in the $12,000 range each month. The market was poor, my decision-making ability no less so.

I had made a huge error in the purchase, as the income proved insufficient to be profitable, and I chose to close the company. I had about fifty rental cars, and when I began sending them to sell at auction, they were bringing hundreds less each than I owed. I started another company, the King Edwards Auto Group, with an Augusta friend and sold the cars one by one to pay the creditor. It was laborious and took more than a year. Older cars in the South at that time were sold with weekly payment contracts; therefore I had to finance many of them.

Compounding my mistake, the modular home company on my property closed its store, a victim of the financial environment. I was now without income and plenty of outgo, another result of 9/11. I decided to use the property to build a self-storage company. I selected a very competent partner who owned many properties and had to give part of my ownership to a San Diego judge in order to make my portion of the down payment and to achieve the credit necessary.

I was able to utilize Bill N. to supervise construction, and the company became successful. After several years, we sold the company and Bill N. and I built a new company in nearby Aiken, South Carolina.

CHAPTER 99

THE AIKEN SOUTH CAROLINA STORAGE COMPANY

We partnered with the original owner of the Augusta property, who put up $250,000. I had paid his note with interest for many years. He had observed Bill's supervision of the Augusta storage company, and he was comfortable with the new partnership. He was chairman of the board of our branch of Sun Trust Bank in Augusta. Our credit was assured. The cash necessary was $987,000. We bought the property, sold a portion, and with the $250,000 from our new partner, and by increasing the mortgage on my and Ginny's home in San Diego, we were able to raise the necessary cash.

An unforeseen situation loomed: Sun Trust was forced by the market upheaval to ask the government to give it the credit necessary to weather the down market. It was among the hundreds of banks to do the same. The governments rules for the "bailout" were to cause a serious problem later.

CHAPTER 100

The construction was an important experience for me as I was hands on during the entire project. Building went well, and the property rented out on schedule according to our original contract.

A problem developed after two years. Our contract called for 80 percent occupancy within twenty-four months. We were at 79 percent at the end of two years, as a result of the down market of 2008. As our partner was chairman of the bank, we felt assured of an extension. It was not to be so.

The 9/11 tragedy caused a serious depression, and Sun Trust had to be bailed out by the government: one of many. As a result, the government had Sun Trust close thirty-seven branches, including the branch in Augusta where we banked.

The closed branches were required to call business loans not on schedule and as we were at 79 percent rather than 80 percent, they could legally call our loan, which they did. The loan was about $2,800,000, and we had never missed a payment. We sued Sun Trust and the lawsuit went on for more than two years.

CHAPTER 101

A NEW DISASTER

Finally, we ran out of options, and Sun Trust put the note for sale to the public for $1,500,000. I called on a friend of mine—I believed him to be a friend—whose family had created and owned an enormous motor home company. He came to Aiken and we spent weeks going over the books and planning. We were to each own a third of the company. My friend was to buy the note from the bank, and we were to finance the note with him. We were to run the company; his only obligation was the financing for which he was to receive 8 percent on the $1,500,000 and one-third of the company.

We spent a month and $10,000 in attorney fees drawing up the agreement. All was well. My "friend" purchased the note from the bank, and the property was now technically his with no legal obligation to include us as outlined in our agreement. We believed we had no reason to bind a contract, of course an enormous mistake. He shut us out, which was totally legal but a serious breach of trust. He offered us a minority situation in the company, but we would have no control and he had shown he could not be trusted.

The bank charged back the balance of the loan to the corporation, which was myself and my partner, about $1,300,000. Our Augusta partner had settled with Sun Trust for an amount over $100,000. This was not an option for Bill N. and me. Bill N. and I then jointly and separately owed more than $1,300,000. My partner was forced to choose bankruptcy, Chapter 7, leaving the debt solely to me.

The practical option was to do the same, which I was forced to elect. Additionally, we lost our share of the loss carried forward allowed by the IRS. Therefore, I had to pay more than $10,000 to the IRS. We were forced to sell our home, whose value had fallen below the amount we owed in the down market, and we could no longer afford the mortgage.

ROBERT EDWARDS

LIFE AFTER BUSINESSES

We were forced to totally rethink our financial situation. Ginny and I were reduced to a retirement income. I was nearly eighty and as a practical matter I was without my old energy and drive, and in fact too old for a new project, nor did I have Ginny's permission to start one. We were therefore forced to readjust our lifestyle to our remaining income.

Our retirement income is modestly adequate. The lessons we have learned in AA allowed us to go beyond resentment toward the former friend who "stole" $987,000 from us. We lived in a beautiful home high above the city of San Diego with a view of the ocean, the city itself, the bay, and Mexico in the distance. People believe we are wealthy, but we are certainly not. We have since downsized to a small condo..

CHAPTER 102

Ginny and I have now been married fifty-three years at this writing and have learned to love and live well. Our defects of character are slowly being removed, first by acceptance of their existence, second by becoming entirely ready for our higher power to remove them. Much of our success in life, nevertheless, has been by living the principles of the AA program, which requires observing a program that includes a power greater than ourselves.

Alcoholics Anonymous has had and is having an enormous influence on our life. You have read some of our history, but let me recount the major differences in our life due to having the balance of our life free of alcohol combined with the tools of recovery.

Over time, we were able to combine mature decision-making, the tools of the AA program, and the spiritual condition of a higher power in our life. These tripled the speed of our recovery. I speak of the slow but deliberate recovery over thirty-five years of sobriety. Remember, I had eighteen years to achieve the situation into which I brought my family into recovery.

As earlier described, our home of more than thirty years had become burdened by liens and the cost of the liens, eventually more than $6,000 each month. Every month I faced the enormous stress of making the monthly payments. I had to put all my energy into earning enough to meet the financial obligation of the mortgage.

Although some of this situation was due to the vicissitudes of life, much more was due to a history of impulsive decisions influenced by a desire for instant gratification. This immaturity was a condition of the disease of alcoholism. These episodes of poor decision-making had a long history. If searching for excuses, I might add ADHD, which includes impulsivity. Overcoming these poor decisions was somewhat balanced by an extremely exceptional ability to recover. Another project would present itself to my mind and often had success. On average we were able to stay afloat financially. I gained financial advantage through experience and above average intelligence.

The combined advantages of recovery and experience allowed some victories, and in time I found myself in highly profitable financial situations, and I had gained a position of respect that yielded certain opportunities. These opportunities involved millions of dollars, which I had become capable to raise. Several were successful, including my final project, the large storage facility in South Carolina. The company had a successful first two years. I had highly competent partners. Alas, the financial collapse of 2008 caused a loss of nearly $500,000. We lost the company and three years.

I was then approaching the age of eighty, with less of the physical and mental ingredients necessary to earn enough to meet those financial requirements easily. There also was little time to start again, and I developed medical problems that gave me an only 1 to 3 percent chance to survive. I obviously did survive and now, with a cardiac implant device, I am doing well except for a little gift from God for smoking for twenty-five years. That gift is COPD, a pulmonary issue that is limiting.

CHAPTER 103

The housing bubble had readjusted home values back to earlier levels. Our home dropped more than $300,000 in value, below our mortgage. Still we fought to keep our home, until a trusted realtor friend counseled Ginny and me with the facts.

He had us put the house on the market on what had come to be called a short sale. The process took months, and he counseled us to put our mortgage payment safely away in cash for the time when we would need to lease a new home. We did so, and the strategy was successful. When the house sold, we were able to have a first and last payment to begin a new life in a new home. Of course, the value of the property has rebounded to more than its original value, but years later.

A new challenge emerged: the cost of renting or leasing a new home was much higher than we could have imagined. Of course we had neither the income nor the credit for a purchase. The average cost of a modest house or apartment large enough for our needs was $2,250 a month, more than half our income, which according to conservative criteria should not exceed one third. We were appalled at prices in our area. Apartments in large complexes required better credit than we had now due to our new financial situation. Another choice was moving from San Diego and away from friends and family.

Incredibly our realtor called a friend who had a home available. We met him at the location. The house was located high above the city in a wonderful area. The owner was in his mid-eighties, was amazingly comfortable financially, and had remodeled his home of eight thousand square feet into two extremely livable areas. The upper area had the spiral staircase from below closed off and he was able to "manage" with "only" six thousand square feet of living space. For a then single eighty-four-year-old man, it was "adequate." The view from the home was of the city, San Diego Bay, the Pacific Ocean, the Point, and Mexico. The upper floor had a two-car garage and more than two thousand feet of living space.

ROBERT EDWARDS

The home was built about fifty years ago by two Mafia brothers. The carpet was two-inch-thick white shag, and the walls opposite the front of the home, which was solid window, was floor-to-ceiling mirrors—exactly everything you would expect from a Mafioso. The story of the Mafia brothers, one of whom was killed by the Mafia, the other placed in a witness protection program, is very entertaining but for another time.

When Ginny saw the house, it took her no more than ten seconds to say we would take it. We gave the owner a check for two months, which due to wise counsel we were able to do easily. Our new monthly obligation was nearly $4,000 less than our mortgage on the home we were forced to sell.

Our new landlord quickly became incredibly pleased with us. I never asked for any repairs to be done I could not do myself. Ginny quickly redecorated the house to many times its original condition. The owner and I are nearly the same age and enjoyed one another; he fed four feral cats and often traveled to Denmark and Russia for weeks at a time, and I fed the cats while he was gone. We lived a very synergistic lifestyle, and, although he could easily get double the rent, he was comfortable with the trade-off. We felt enormously blessed. We were there more than three years. Unfortunately, the owner was seriously injured in an auto accident and the estate sold the home. We were forced to downsize.

Fortunately, our growth, particularly mine, has put Ginny and me on the same page. I have overcome my inability to communicate with Ginny. Now I share my thoughts with her before I commit us to a plan of action—new behavior for me. Our children now have come back to us; they had kept a comfortable distance from me, which kept them from their mother as well. They can now trust me and our relationship with them has improved. We now talk to them most days and support each other beautifully. Birthdays and holidays are usually spent together. Our sobriety has also influenced their sobriety. Our youngest daughter had fourteen years clean and sober until an accumulation of physical problems took her life at age forty-one. Our oldest son has celebrated nine years of sobriety in AA. He had been electrocuted and his rehabilitation had him on enormous doses of a dangerous pain medication, oxycodone, to which he had become addicted. He is now drug free, including all pain meds, and pain free. Our second son reacted to our alcoholism by not drinking except moderately. He, however, became interested in the psychology of our disease and in the general profession of psychology, and is soon to be licensed as a family life therapist.

We have been part of a couple's recovery program, Couples in Recovery, for the entire period of our recovery. Our marriage is as a result amazingly successful. We are completely happy and content. Although we now spend nearly half our income on our home, the sacrifice is, to us, worth it. We have had many AA and church events in our home: potlucks, couples' meetings, Bible studies, and church parties, especially before we downsized. In other words, we can spend little on outside entertainment, but are repaid by the pleasure of our home, our friends, our church, and our recovery programs. There is no question that the credit for our success is the AA program and as described in Steps 1 and 2, *a higher power*.

CHAPTER 104

MORE ABOUT OUR ALCOHOLICS ANONYMOUS PROGRAM AND A HIGHER POWER

A common theme in all that has been reported about AA is one alcoholic talking to another and service in many forms in a spiritual program. How are Ginny and I repaying our debt to the program and to the faith?

I started a meeting that is now more than thirty-three years old; it has made sobriety possible for hundreds, although it may have done for me more than it has for others. Ginny and I sponsor, a pleasure for which again we receive more than we give; we have answered the telephone at AA Central, led meetings, made coffee, and been of service in many other ways.

Ginny and I have served as elders at our church and additionally I have served as a deacon. We now serve as ushers, although at this writing, we are in the COVID-19 pandemic and church services are not possible.

Are we unusual, or not at all? We are members of a fellowship that shares the responsibility of keeping the doors open and are merely doing our share for which we are amply compensated in love, friendship, and health. We join others in more than sixty thousand groups in the United States alone. Alcoholics Anonymous has spawned many other twelve-step groups such as Narcotics Anonymous, Debtors Anonymous, Gamblers Anonymous, and others too numerous to list here. Alcoholics Anonymous groups exist in 181 countries. The similarity of all meetings everywhere is amazing. You can visit a meeting anywhere in the world and feel at home. I have personally observed and have been told by those who have visited meetings where other languages are spoken, and you can benefit from the similarity without understanding the language.

The creation of AA is in the top eighty-eight events in importance during the past century. Its value is difficult to evaluate. The alcoholic's drinking affects eight others on average, and his or her recovery also affects that same number.

CHAPTER 105

THE "GOD THING"

An important characteristic of the initial difficulty with the AA program is the acceptance of the fact that AA is a spiritual program. To most, spirituality refers to God, and to many, if not most, recovering alcoholics, God is an exceedingly difficult issue, especially in the early time in our recovery.

When *Alcoholics Anonymous* was written, the first draft contained many references to God. It so offended, or perhaps frightened, so many of the first members, mostly atheists and agnostics, that they compelled Bill W. to go back through the book and change references to God to "God as you understood Him" and as "a power greater than ourselves," or merely "a higher power." He did so in a three-day marathon, and it may have allowed millions who had overpowering difficulty with God to come into the program without first having to overcome the "stigma" of God in their mind. *This issue has come to be known as the "God Thing."*

The view of God held by the incoming members of AA was varied. Many came from families with a firm belief in the Christian God. Some came from families with no belief in any god. Most came from families with a belief in a god but with little observance of a "worship" of the god of their belief. Others came with a view of a higher power, not the Christian God. Most came with the feeling that their lifestyle put them beyond the purview of the previous god of their belief had for them.

CHAPTER 106

MORE ON MY "GOD THING"

My background consists of a Baptist upbringing in rural Texas with moderate church participation in various church services. Therefore, my belief was imposed on me by family dynamics. As a child, I did not disbelieve in God nor did I concern myself as to whether there was a god or whether that god was the "True God."

Left to my own devices in high school, I drifted away from childhood-imposed Christian beliefs, and as I went to college and began independently thinking about "God," I became more agnostic in my thinking, perhaps even atheistic. Perhaps I thought it was cool. As I became a drinker, "God" became less and less important as my behavior deteriorated as a result of my developing alcoholism. I made an unconscious decision to become an atheist. Upon reflection, I have come to believe this "atheism" was having an egoist persona rather than having lost all my belief in the Christian God. In other words, I may have thought it was cool to be an atheist. I had become someone who teased everyone who said they were Christian, especially those who would proselyte me. This had become my persona.

This would change after a "spiritual experience" I was to have, which would reintroduce me to church involvement. This would also introduce me into several years of nondrinking. This nondrinking, as I have written, did not involve AA and I drank again and left the church, probably as I did not believe the activities could coexist.

CHAPTER 107

MY NEW ATTITUDES TOWARD GOD

Now, thirty-five years later, I have with clarity of sobriety, began to draw conclusions over the dynamics of my rethinking of my attitudes and beliefs of God. My conclusions are shared by Albert Einstein, although a noted atheist, who said, *"The most important function of art and science is to awaken the cosmic religious feeling that keep it alive."*

Hazelden's "Touchstones," "Daily Meditations for Men," adds, "There is no need to be concerned about a conflict between science and the spiritual life. People have turned to the spiritual in many ways since the beginning of humanity. Some are tribal and primitive, some very emotional, some focused on ideas and philosophy, some centered on tradition. Perhaps in the very center of our humanness is a spiritual compass [conscience]. When we disown that orientation, do we lose some of our humanness? This program [AA] did not invent the spiritual outlook. It only tells us recovery will come through awakening of the spiritual within us."

"We are on an exploration," Hazelden continues, "We give ourselves over to it and only discover where our awakening will lead us as it unfolds. The Steps [of AA] tell us to engage with the god of our understanding, to develop a relationship of trust, total openness, and humility, and to improve their contact. As the center of our humanness is restored, we come alive and our daily tasks take on new meaning."

After several decades of the study of more than eighteen books daily, and now twenty-one or more, in each morning of meditation includes a combination of AA, Al-Anon, psychology, science, religious books, and the Bible, I have reached a new level of thinking.

Einstein also said, *"The significant problems we have cannot be solved by the same level of thinking with which we created them."* Does that mean that the thinking that got us into this situation cannot get us out? We may have doubts of

God's very existence; however, it is not the god of faith we are doubting, but perhaps the god of our limited experience. In my story, you should have observed the length of my road less traveled, and also the wisdom while on the road and those secrets I have encountered.

CHAPTER 108

OTHER THINKERS

Today we are aware of the existence of many universes, more than the grains of sand on the beach. The Hubble Telescope has demonstrated that fact beyond question. Isaac Newton (1643–1727), the father of physics famous for the law of gravity and the foremost scientific thinker of his time, believed *the universe was confined in a box, a large rectangle; to Newton infinity was too difficult a concept to express.*

Albert Einstein regarded himself as an agnostic who admired some Christian views but said a personal god was a concept he could not accept. His attitude was of humility corresponding to the weakness of our intellectual understanding of nature and ourselves. Einstein was also quoted as saying, *"The deep emotional conviction of the presence of a superior reasoning power, which is revealed in the incomprehensible universe, forms my idea of god."*

This corresponds with the thoughts of Isaiah, a prophet in the Old Testament, who, we are cautioned, wrote that God told him: *"For my thoughts are not your thoughts, neither are my ways your ways. As the heavens are higher than the earth, so are my ways higher than your ways and my thoughts than your thoughts."* I have come to believe that if you could understand God and God's ways, *He could not be great enough to be God.*

I agree with Herbert Spencer, who said, *"There is a principle which is a bar against all information, which is a proof against all arguments, and which cannot fail to keep a man in everlasting ignorance; that principle is contempt prior to investigation."* In agreement with Spencer, I determined to study the Bible in order to understand it to the limit of my ability. I do not consider myself an expert, yet I have found an amazing sameness in all the material I have studied in the Bible, the AA program, science, and philosophy: *doing the right thing, simple enough, not at all complex. Christianity: do unto others… Have a belief in God or a higher power. If we all loved one another, could the world be in the condition it is in today? Even the 10 Commandments might contribute to a peaceful world. I include the nonreligious items. Do not murder. Do not commit adultery. Do not steal. Do not bear false witness. Do not covet.*

There is that "God Thing" again!

I have come to believe God is not a puppeteer who pulls the strings on his creation, but who created an order that, if followed, allows a perfectly orderly life that permits you to view every occurrence in your life as having occurred without God's interference but having been set into motion in creation. *This is merely where my thinking has me at this time, and with an open mind I would prefer not knowing what God will not reveal to me.* I also believe everything that happens in life is a lesson that forms who we are.

CHAPTER 109

AFTER CONSIDERATION, HOW DO YOU CHOOSE WHETHER OR NOT TO BELIEVE IN GOD?

There lives more faith in honest doubt, believe me

than in half the creeds.

Alfred Lord Tennyson

Let us first recognize we are on the earth. The earth is a planet in our solar system, one of eight. All revolve around the sun. The earth's orbit is one year. The sun provides the temperature on the earth which, on average, is 61 degrees Fahrenheit. However, as the earth's orbit is elliptical, the distance from the sun changes, giving us summer and winter.

The earth rotates around the sun. Therefore, much of the time the earth faces the sun, but the balance of the time the sun is hidden. Since the sun is our light source, this gives us day and night. The sun is a solar system, of which there may be 100 billion. Five hundred are charted. Mars is another planet in our solar system. Mars is 141.39 million miles from the earth. Nevertheless, the solar system is so precise our government sent a rocket to Mars and landed it in a predetermined crater. The trip took seven months.

What is the point? The point is this: can this be without design? Or can there be a higher power from which a design came? Is there a higher power, or has this celestial design occurred by an amazing accident? Blaise Pascal, a seventeenth-century philosopher, mathematician, and physicist said: "A pragmatic reason for believing in God: even under the assumption that God's existence is unlikely, the potential benefits of believing are so vast as to make betting on theism rational."

Actually, either asks for amazing acceptance of an extraordinary choice. Of course, I could also pose the question of an acorn dropping from a tree and becoming an oak tree from which a seed drips and becomes an oak tree. Or of the birth of a child who becomes a parent and has a child. The child becomes a parent. Actually, I could offer other options. Nevertheless,

one choice is explained by the Bible. The other leaves the choice to you and is one of a scientific option, of which there are many.

Prophecy is history written in advance. The Bible is 28 percent prophecy. Dr. John Walvoord, dean of Dallas Theological Seminary, teaches that half of one thousand prophecies documented in the Bible have been fulfilled in the past century.

The option offered in the Bible asks for acceptance of many facts. Nevertheless, to me, after many decades, the choice became clear. Also, the benefits vary greatly. God gives you free will in your choice. Choose well.

CHAPTER 110

WHY IT WORKS

AN OPINION

More than a century ago alcoholism was thought of as choice. In 1956, alcoholism was designated a disease by the AMA. This enabled insurance companies, or more exactly, required them, to treat alcoholism as a disease and to pay for its treatment; thus, the birth of alcohol treatment centers such as the Betty Ford Center.

To explain alcoholism, let me use metaphorically a smoking addiction. If you ever smoked, you may recall the first cigarette probably made you very dizzy—at least it had a strong effect on you, the next one less so, and so on. What happened? There are 50 million nicotine addicts in the United States, and one of five deaths results from smoking. It is the leading preventable cause of death. Why, then, do people smoke? Peer pressure is probably the cause of most to start smoking. Why, with the empirical truth of the dangers of smoking, do not they quit?

Why continue smoking when most people have knowledge of these facts?

Most new smokers are teens, an age during which people feel indestructible. Nicotine, the primary addictive agent in cigarettes, is absorbed into the bloodstream and within ten to twenty seconds reaches the brain, causing the brain to release endorphins and creating a "buzz" of pleasure and energy.

The "buzz" quickly fades and leaves you feeling tired, let down, and wanting to recreate those sensations; thus, you have a desire to have another cigarette. The body, however, builds a tolerance to nicotine, and you must smoke more and more for the original effect. This causes three out of four teen smokers to become adult smokers.

Much the same thing happens with alcohol. In moderation, the effects of alcohol can make you more socially relaxed, talk more easily, make you livelier, and thus "more fun." Every successful social drinker is aware of these facts. The unsuccessful social drinker also is aware of these facts, but too often avoids using this knowledge. Unfortunately, the body develops a tolerance to alcohol and the sense of wellness becomes elusive, causing some to chase this illusion to the extent of overcoming the body's ability to tolerate the amounts of alcohol consumed—alcoholism.

To overcome this tolerance, the body asks for more and more alcohol until the mental and physical processes will not enable you to act in an appropriate manner. Automobile wrecks, abusive behaviors, and other accidents become common. Improper use of your income to satisfy this abuse occurs. As important, the reduced ability to maintain a responsible lifestyle affects eight other people, primarily in the family, the workplace, and friendships. Also, the eight others impact several others. With the effects of maintaining an alcoholic lifestyle, such as missing work, affairs, and inability to pay one's obligations, life deteriorates to the loss of the home and family, and eventually to hospitalization and even death. Yet, similar to the one out of five deaths that are smoking related (nearly five hundred thousand annually), alcohol accounts for eighty-eight thousand deaths annually, sixty-two thousand men and twenty-six thousand women; alcohol is fourth leading preventable cause of death in the United States.

Additionally, alcohol-impaired driving fatalities account for another 9,967 deaths (31 percent of overall driving fatalities). Nevertheless, despite all those losses, people continue to abuse alcohol. Again, why? The body has developed an addiction to alcohol and the body's call for alcohol has overcome reason.

Is this a new problem? Historically there has always been the town drunk; recall all the old movies, especially Westerns, where there was always a person known as the town drunk. It was always a man, usually peaceful and well tolerated with some affection. There was never any attempt to get him sober. Doctors were without solutions. The religious men were as unsuccessful. There were few physiatrists and those with experience believed only a spiritual event would work. Some sort of psychic change was necessary, according to world-famous psychiatrist Carl Jung, but no one understood how to produce this psychic change.

In 1934, Dr. William Silkworth, while treating Bill Wilson, cofounder of AA, for the third time, was forced to tell Bill's wife there was nothing to be done for him; he would die or be committed to an insane asylum. Bill overheard this conversation, and although he was not at all religious, told God he would do anything to get well. This is when Bill W. had his famous "white light" experience.

This met the need for a spiritual experience and psychic change. But what about the "allergy" of the body that we now understand to be the chemical changes brought about by the abuse of alcohol? The "God Thing" gains strength because new men and women join the program and immediately lose the desire to drink, some with no withdrawal symptoms. Withdrawal is sometimes so difficult that many must undergo being medically withdrawn.

Enter now the series of events we have come to know as the "God Thing." By one alcoholic talking to another alcoholic a few alcoholics were able to get sober. They banded together and in a group were able to share their story. They found they were not alone. The healing "is in the hearing," a simple yet important truth experienced in these meetings. They heard there was an allergy of the body and a disorder of the mind. *A dozen meetings would make all you have read more believable.*

Hearing others' experiences and shared emotions, the newly recovering alcoholics gained understanding that they were not alone. The personal witness of the growth of others gave them hope. At first, they may have simply believed that others believed. Today, major cities have hundreds of meeting every day. In San Diego, there are more than one thousand each week. It is impossible not to experience the empirical truth that recovery is possible if you experience a sufficient number of meetings and have a sincere desire to stop drinking. *Members suddenly become aware the urge to drink is leaving them.*

What, then, about the "allergy" of the body as described by Dr. Silkworth? This is a physical matter, and withdrawal from chemicals causes serious physical symptoms by the body readjusting to the lack of the chemicals previously in the synapse. The successful recovery of some alcoholics in AA, having quit alcohol immediately upon entering the program and yet not experiencing withdrawal symptoms, at least to the extent expected, is occasionally experienced. This phenomenon is not explained by medicine; we accept it as a *"God Thing."* Why it works is a mystery psychiatrically, medically, and religiously, yet today millions are living sober successfully.

But, again, what is sobriety? Sobriety, to most of the population, is simply not drinking. Not drinking, however, can be accomplished without sobriety. Simply not drinking, in the AA program, is termed by some as being dry. Sobriety is much more complex than simply not drinking. Not drinking can be accomplished, by some, by a simple decision to stop drinking, for whatever reasoning is compelling to the drinker. *Alcoholics Anonymous was recognized as the eighty-eighth most important event of the past century. To some, achieving sobriety is of this magnitude.* As soon as the chemical or emotional balance is lost when the body absorbs the chemical, the nervous system, at the area where the billions of connectors, called axons, calls for a replacement for the chemical necessary to reestablish the balance. *This call for a balance is termed an addiction to that product or chemical.* A similar but more complex process occurs when the body calls for a drink of alcohol or another drug.

A SOLUTION AND HOW TO START

Reason dictates that whenever drinking is causing problems in the home, the workplace, the ability to adapt to everyday situations, a solution must be found, thus this study. These issues are influenced by genetics, but also include acquired defects of character, chemical abnormalities, and issues of environment. These issues and others are principally responsible for the disease of alcoholism. Attaining sobriety is complex and difficult. The secrets of sobriety come slowly on the road to recovery, as recovery requires the complete examination of the self.

The recovery rate is not high as addiction is strong.

The alcoholic also must understand the problems in order to contemplate the solution. The AA program suggests that to do so one must do a "thorough and moral inventory" of oneself. This inventory is included as a paraphrase of Step 4 from the *Big Book of Alcoholics Anonymous*, and the inventory is necessary in order to understand the road ahead of us. The *Big Book* and the twelve steps advised therein have been discussed in detail in the body of this book.

Scott Peck, again, would call the road to recovery "*a road less traveled.*"

The objective of this book has been to reveal these secrets of sobriety I have learned in the more than thirty-five years of my recovery. The extent of my recovery does not include all the secrets of sobriety, I am sure, as I have constantly improved my own understanding. These secrets will hopefully have been revealed in the review of my life, my alcoholism, my recovery, and what I have learned.

Years ago, I believed I had discovered the secret of not drinking. The secret—singular. I now understand the secrets of sobriety are on a continuum: a continuum is a coherent whole characterized as a collection, sequence, or progression of values varying by minute degrees as defined by Merriam Webster. I have learned these secrets, as I have needed the understanding of these secrets to remain sober, on a continuum. Therefore, it is on a continuum from not taking that first drink, to a solid understanding of the process, that should have revealed to a patient reader with a sincere interest in sobriety, those secrets. Others shall have lost interest. Therefore, I have chosen to use my own story of recovery in order to personalize and reveal my own bias and character defects, to an understanding of the author. I trust it has been useful.

The secrets may have become apparent as they occur in the story of my recovery. These building blocks were, from day one of my recovery to today, with more than thirteen thousand days without alcohol, critical to a totally different life from that experienced during "my disease."

During my own "road less traveled," I developed a strong curiosity about AA, how it works, and how it come into being, so much so that I obtained a bachelor's degree in alcohol and drug counseling. Much of my education is included in this narrative. In these pages, I have attempted to describe these secrets of sobriety and additionally the steps necessary to understand and utilize these secrets in your own life, if sobriety is indeed your goal.

I have said that every day I learn more. Why, therefore, if I am experiencing continual learning, have I not put this book off until I have it all? Quite simply, my younger brother just passed from COVID-19, and I realized this may have been my last chance.

REWARDS

My own reward, to my amazement, has been a high degree of serenity in my life with my wife of more than fifty years, my children, my church, my God, and my programs. I have attempted to give an understanding of these secrets by taking you on the journey of my life, my introduction to AA, my growth as it occurred, and an introduction to how AA began, and some of the important people and events in its growth and maturity.

The significant problems we have encountered cannot be solved by the same level of thinking with which we created them.

Albert Einstein

I HOPE THE JOURNEY HAS BEEN SUCCESSFUL

I began this story with this statement: "I am an eighty-five-year-old alcoholic." But also,

"I was a nine-year-old boy as World War II ended."

A freshman in a school with only four seniors and no college preparation.

A senior in a border town with Mexico and fifteen-cent whisky.

A college freshman with no college preparation.

...ght training in the United States Air Force Cadet program.

My first major disaster, elimination from the flight program.

A new life, mixed with alcohol and life experiences, both positive and negative.

A different life, one without alcohol, and with a new approach.

These challenges have been met, with splendid results.

Nevertheless, the price has been consuming.

I have no problems, my life is complete, I am surrounded by love, serenity is mine.

This book is written, I dare not add another line. I must contribute that which I am now able, or it may be all forever lost.

The price is paid. I am content.